SŪRAT AL-ANʿĀM

with translations, transliterations, & accompanying duas

Daybreak Press
3533 Lexington Avenue North, Arden Hills, MN 55126
www.rabata.org/daybreakpress | daybreakpress@rabata.org

ISBN (print): 978-1-967369-06-5
ISBN (ebook): 978-1-967369-07-2
LCCN: 2025946280

Cover design: Zainab Arshad | Zainabmade.com
Typesetting: Islam Farid | islamfarid.net

Printed in the United States of America

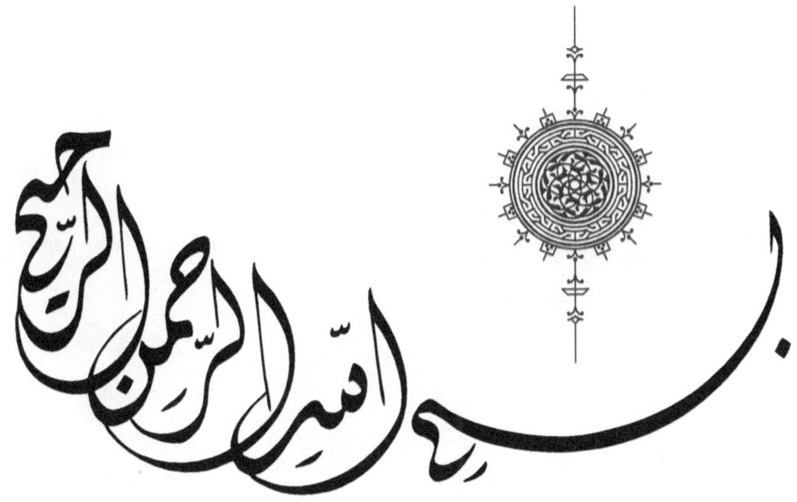
بسم الله الرحمن الرحيم

Publisher's Note

The translations of the Quran used in this book are from Mustafa Khattab's *The Clear Quran*, with adaptations based on the needs of the audience.

The transliteration is based on the IJMES system of transliteration, but has been adapted to make the Arabic easier to pronounce. For example, letters that appear in the Arabic text but are silent in pronunciation have been deleted from the transliteration. The table below shows the English letter or symbol that corresponds to each Arabic letter or sound.

Consonants				Vowels	
ʾ	ء	ḍ	ض	a	◌́
b	ب	ṭ	ط	u	◌
t	ت	ẓ	ظ	i	◌
th	ث	ʿ	ع		
j	ج	gh	غ	an	◌
ḥ	ح	f	ف	un	◌
kh	خ	q	ق	in	◌
d	د	k	ك		
dh	ذ	l	ل	ā	أَ
r	ر	m	م	ū	وُ
z	ز	n	ن	ī	يِ
s	س	h	ه		
sh	ش	w	و	ay	يَ
ṣ	ص	y	ي	aw	وَ

Contents

Foreword

by Anse Dr. Tamara Gray

Sūrat al-Anʿām is a majestic and powerful chapter, revealed all at once as a single revelation. Ibn ʿAbbās said, "Sūrat al-Anʿām was revealed in Mecca at night, all at once, surrounded by seventy thousand angels who were engaged in the glorification of God."[1] It was the first long sura revealed in Mecca and addressed early Meccan concerns—so many of which are still concerns today. The sura addresses the central truths of *tawḥīd* (divine oneness), *rubūbiyya* (Lordship), and the reality of prophethood and revelation. It is a sura that shatters idols—physical, social, and internal—and reorients the human being toward sincere devotion to Allah alone. It includes refutation of prevalent superstitions, responses to objections, and the uplifting of fundamental moral principles necessary to build a positive culture and society.

The verses of this sura invite both awe and intimacy. They offer arguments for the intellect and nourishment for the soul. As you read, you will encounter reminders of Allah's creation, His sustaining power, and the fate of those who turn away from truth. With every verse, there is an opportunity to respond—to pause, reflect, and whisper back a prayer.

---

[1] *ʿUmdat al-tafsīr*, vol. 1, p. 761, grade: *ṣaḥīḥ*.

The included *dua* are part of a long tradition of *dua* made in accompaniment with Surat al-Anʿām, offering words of praise, gratitude, repentance, and hope. They are to be read along with the sura, not as commentary, but as spiritual responses—moments of turning inward and upward, allowing the heart to speak as the Quran speaks. Ḥudhayfa ibn al-Yamān (may Allah be pleased with them both), said:

> I prayed with the Prophet ﷺ [2] one night, and he began with Sūrat al-Baqara. I said to myself: He will bow at the hundredth verse. Then he continued, and I said: He will complete it in one rakʿa. Then he continued, and I said: He will bow with it. Then he began Sūrat al-Nisāʾ and recited it. Then he began Sūrat Āl ʿImrān and recited it—he was reciting slowly and deliberately. When he passed by a verse that contained glorification (*tasbīḥ*), he glorified [Allah]. When he passed by a verse of supplication (*suʾāl*), he asked. And when he passed by a verse of seeking refuge (*taʿawwudh*), he sought refuge. [3]

The scholars of *fiqh* have differed as to whether one should make *dua* during prayer (as this narration indicates that the Prophet ﷺ did), or if it is only recommended while reciting Quran. Scholars of the Shafiʿi school have ruled that we can make *dua* (in the way of the Prophet) in response to the Quran during the

---

[2] Hereafter, ﷺ: *ṣallā Allāhu ʿalayhi wa sallam* ("peace and blessings be upon him [the Prophet Muhammad]").

[3] *Ṣaḥīḥ Muslim.*

prayer, while the Hanafi school differs and classifies it as disliked. All schools agree, however, on the importance of responding to the Quran while reciting it outside of prayer with heartfelt devotions.

In a similar vein, Muhammad ibn Ka'b said, "Whomever the Quran reaches, it is as if Allah is speaking to him."[4] And Imam al-Ghazali commented on his words, saying, "If that is presumed, let him not take the formal study of the Quran as his main task. Rather, let him recite as a servant reads the book of his Master, who has written it for him to meditate upon and to act upon what it requires."[5]

The *duas* in this booklet allow your recitation to become a dialogue, a *dhikr*, a spiritual ascent. Let your eyes fill with the beauty of the words, your heart tremble, and your soul recommit to its purpose. And if you remember us while reciting, include us in your blessed *duas*.

Whether you are reading alone or in a group, in Arabic or in translation, we pray this booklet becomes a means of deepening your relationship with the Quran and with the Sustainer of all that is. May your recitation of Sūrat al-Anʿām be filled with light, and may these *dua* become echoes of your own longing, sincerity, and submission.

اللَّهُمَّ اجْعَلْنَا مِنْ أَهْلِ الْقُرْآنِ وَاجْعَلِ الْقُرْآنَ رَبِيعَ قُلُوبِنَا وَنُورَ صُدُورِنَا وَجَلَاءَ أَحْزَانِنَا وَذَهَابَ هُمُومِنَا وَرَفِيقَنَا فِي قُبُورِنَا وَشَفِيعَنَا يَوْمَ نَلْقَاكَ.

Ya Allah, make us the people of the Quran, and make the Quran the spring of our hearts, the light of our chests, the softening of our sadness, the release of our concern, our companion in the grave, and an intercessor for us on the day we meet You.

---

4 *Tafsīr al-Thaʿlabī*, 6:19.

5 *Iḥyāʾ ʿulūm al-dīn*, 1/285.

The Names of Allah

Before reciting Sūrat al-An‘ām, consider reciting the beautiful names of Allah for the fulfillment and alleviation of important concerns.

Begin by reciting the following prayer 10 times.

بِسْمِ اللّٰهِ الرَّحْمَنِ الرَّحِيمِ

سَيِّدِي أَدْخِلْنِي فِي رِيَاضِ أَسْمَائِكَ وَالْبَابِ الَّذِي لَا يُحْجَبُ بِنُورٍ وَلَا بِظُلْمَةٍ وَلَا بِشَـيْءٍ مِنْهُ وَلَا بِشَـيْءٍ خَارِجٍ عَنْهُ وَأَطْلِقْ بِي فِي نَيْلِ النِّعْمَةِ وَارْزُقْنِي رِزْقَ كُلِّ مَرْزُوقٍ حَتَّى أَكُونَ لَكَ فِيكَ وَأَكُونَ فِيكَ لَكَ مُبْتَهِجًا بِحَلَاوَةِ ذَلِكَ مِنْكَ إِنَّكَ عَطُوفٌ كَرِيمٌ.

﴿ مَّا يَفْتَحِ ٱللَّهُ لِلنَّاسِ مِن رَّحْمَةٍ فَلَا مُمْسِكَ لَهَا وَمَا يُمْسِكْ فَلَا مُرْسِلَ لَهُۥ مِنْ بَعْدِهِۦ وَهُوَ ٱلْعَزِيزُ ٱلْحَكِيمُ ﴾

وَصَلَّى اللّٰهُ عَلَى مُحَمَّدٍ وَعَلَى آلِهِ وَصَحْبِهِ وَسَلَّمَ.

Bismillāhir Raḥmānir Raḥīm

Sayyidī, adkhilnī fī riyāḍi asmā’ika wal-bābi-lladhī lā yuḥjabu binūrin wa-lā bi-ẓulmatin wa-lā bishay’in minhu wa-lā bishay’in khārijin ‘anhu wa-aṭliq bī fī naylin-ni‘mati wa-rzuqnī rizqa kulli marzūqin ḥattā akūna laka fīka wa-akūna fīka laka mubtahijan bi-ḥalāwati dhālika minka innaka ‘aṭūfun karīm.

Mā yaftaḥi-llāhu lin-nāsi mir-raḥmatin fa-lā mumsika lahā, wa-mā yumsik fa-lā mursila lahu min ba‘dih; wa-huwal-‘Azīzul-Ḥakīm.

Wa-ṣalla-Allāhu ‘alā Muḥammadin wa-‘alā ālih wa-ṣaḥbihi wa-sallam.

In the name of Allah, the Merciful, the Compassionate

My Lord, permit me to enter the gardens of Your names, into the gate that is not concealed by light or darkness, nor by anything external to it. And move me toward the acquisition of Your blessings and provide me the provision of every person to whom You have provided, that I may be of those who are dedicated to You and through You, and that I may be joyful in my presence with You, from the sweetness that comes from You. You are the Subtle, the Forgiving, the Generous.

❧ *Any mercy Allah grants, no one can withhold, and any that Allah withholds, none can release it other than Him. And Allah is the Glorious, the Wise.* ❧

And may Allah send prayers and peace upon Prophet Muhammad and his family and his companions.

Now make *dua* for what you wish to ask for, and follow it with your recitation of the names. Your *dua* will, with the permission of Allah, be accepted and responded to.

The Names

	Translation	Transliteration	Arabic
1	O He who is Allah, the One who there is no god but He	*Yā man huwa-Allāhul-ladhī lā ilāha illā huwa*	يَا مَنْ هُوَ اللَّهُ الَّذِي لَا إِلَـهَ إِلَّا هُوَ
2	The Most Compassionate	*ar-Raḥmān*	الرَّحْمَـنُ
3	The Most Merciful	*ar-Raḥīm*	الرَّحِيمُ
4	The King	*al-Malik*	المَلِكُ
5	The Holy	*al-Quddūs*	القُدُّوسُ
6	The Peaceful	*as-Salām*	السَّلَامُ
7	The Source of Faith	*al-Mu'min*	المُؤْمِنُ
8	The Overseeing Guardian	*al-Muhaymin*	المُهَيْمِنُ
9	The Glorious	*al-'Azīz*	العَزِيزُ
10	The Compeller, the Restorer	*al-Jabbār*	الجَبَّارُ

11	The Supreme, the Majestic	*al-Mutakabbir*	المُتَكَبِّرُ
12	The Creator	*al-Khāliq*	الخَالِقُ
13	The Originator	*al-Bāri'*	البَارِئُ
14	The Fashioner	*al-Muṣawwir*	المُصَوِّرُ
15	The Ever Forgiving	*al-Ghaffār*	الغَفَّارُ
16	The Subduer	*al-Qahhār*	القَهَّارُ
17	The Bestower	*al-Wahhāb*	الوَهَّابُ
18	The Provider	*ar-Razzāq*	الرَّزَّاقُ
19	The Opener	*al-Fattāḥ*	الفَتَّاحُ
20	The All-Knowing	*al-ʿAlīm*	العَلِيمُ
21	The Collector	*al-Qābiḍ*	القَابِضُ
22	The Expander	*al-Bāsiṭ*	البَاسِطُ
23	The Reducer, the Abaser	*al-Khāfiḍ*	الخَافِضُ
24	The Exalter, the One who Elevates	*ar-Rāfiʿ*	الرَّافِعُ
25	The Honorer, the Bestower	*al-Muʿizz*	المُعِزُّ
26	The Subduer	*al-Mudhill*	المُذِلُّ

27	The All-Hearing	as-Samī'	السَّمِيعُ
28	The All-Seeing	al-Baṣīr	البَصِيرُ
29	The Ultimate Judge	al-Ḥakam	الحَكَمُ
30	The Utterly Just	al-'Adl	العَدْلُ
31	The Most Gentle	al-Laṭīf	اللَّطِيفُ
32	The All-Aware	al-Khabīr	الخَبِيرُ
33	The Most Forbearing	al-Ḥalīm	الحَلِيمُ
34	The Great, the Supreme	al-'Aẓīm	العَظِيمُ
35	The Forgiving	al-Ghafūr	الغَفُورُ
36	The Most Appreciative	ash-Shakūr	الشَّكُورُ
37	The Most High, the Exalted	al-'Alīyy	العَلِيُّ
38	The Greatest, the Most Grand	al-Kabīr	الكَبِيرُ
39	The Preserver	al-Ḥafīẓ	الحَفِيظُ
40	The Sustainer, the Maintainer	al-Muqīt	المُقِيتُ
41	The Reckoner	al-Ḥasīb	الحَسِيبُ

42	The Sublime, the Majestic	al-Jalīl	الجَلِيلُ
43	The Most Generous	al-Karīm	الكَرِيمُ
44	The Ever Watchful	ar-Raqīb	الرَّقِيبُ
45	The Responder	al-Mujīb	المُجِيبُ
46	The All-Encompassing, the Boundless	al-Wāsiʿ	الوَاسِعُ
47	The All-Wise	al-Ḥakīm	الحَكِيمُ
48	The Most Loving	al-Wadūd	الوَدُودُ
49	The Most Glorious	al-Majīd	المَجِيدُ
50	The Resurrector	al-Bāʿith	البَاعِثُ
51	The All-Observing, the Witnessing	ash-Shahīd	الشَّهِيدُ
52	The Absolute Truth	al-Ḥaqq	الحَقُّ
53	The Trustee, the Disposer of Affairs	al-Wakīl	الوَكِيلُ
54	The Strong	al-Qawiyy	القَوِيُّ
55	The Firm, the Steadfast	al-Matīn	المَتِينُ
56	The Protecting Ally	al-Waliyy	الوَلِيُّ

57	The Praiseworthy	al-Ḥamīd	الْحَمِيدُ
58	The All-Enumerating, the One who Counts	al-Muḥṣī	الْمُحْصِي
59	The Originator, the Initiator	al-Mubdi'	الْمُبْدِئُ
60	The Restorer, the Reinstater	al-Muʿīd	الْمُعِيدُ
61	The Giver of Life	al-Muḥyī	الْمُحْيِي
62	The Creator of Death	al-Mumīt	الْمُمِيتُ
63	The Ever Living	al-Ḥayy	الْحَيُّ
64	The Sustainer, the Self-Subsisting	al-Qayyūm	الْقَيُّومُ
65	The Perceiver	al-Wājid	الْوَاجِدُ
66	The Illustrious, the Magnificent	al-Mājid	الْمَاجِدُ
67	The One, the Indivisible	al-Wāḥid	الْوَاحِدُ
68	The Unique, the One	al-Aḥad	الْأَحَدُ
69	The Eternal, the Satisfier of Needs	aṣ-Ṣamad	الصَّمَدُ
70	The Able, the Omnipotent	al-Qādir	الْقَادِرُ

71	The Powerful	al-Muqtadir	الْمُقْتَدِرُ
72	The Expediter, the Promoter	al-Muqaddim	الْمُقَدِّمُ
73	The Delayer	al-Mu'akhkhir	الْمُؤَخِّرُ
74	The First	al-Awwal	الْأَوَّلُ
75	The Last, the Utmost	al-Ākhir	الْآخِرُ
76	The Manifest	az̧-Z̧āhir	الظَّاهِرُ
77	The Hidden, the Knower of the Hidden	al-Bāt̤in	الْبَاطِنُ
78	The Sole Governor	al-Wālī	الْوَالِي
79	The Most Exalted	al-Muta'ālī	الْمُتَعَالِي
80	The Source of All Goodness	al-Barr	الْبَرُّ
81	The Ever Pardoning, the Accepter of Repentance	at-Tawwāb	التَّوَّابُ
82	The Avenger	al-Muntaqim	الْمُنْتَقِمُ
83	The Pardoner	al-'Afuww	الْعَفُوُّ
84	The Most Kind	ar-Ra'ūf	الرَّؤُوفُ
85	The King of the Kingdom	Mālikul-Mulk	مَالِكُ الْمُلْكِ

86	The Lord of Majesty and Bounty	*Dhūl-Jalāli wal-Ikrām*	ذُو الجَلَالِ وَالإِكْرَامِ
87	The Equitable	*al-Muqsiṭ*	المُقْسِطُ
88	The Gatherer, the Uniter	*al-Jāmi'*	الجَامِعُ
89	The Self-Sufficient, the Wealthy	*al-Ghaniyy*	الغَنِيُّ
90	The Enricher	*al-Mughnī*	المُغْنِي
91	The Withholder	*al-Māni'*	المَانِعُ
92	The Distresser	*aḍ-Ḍārr*	الضَّارُّ
93	The Benefactor	*an-Nāfi'*	النَّافِعُ
94	The Light	*an-Nūr*	النُّورُ
95	The Guide	*al-Hādī*	الهَادِي
96	The Incomparable Originator	*al-Badī'*	البَدِيعُ
97	The Everlasting	*al-Bāqī*	البَاقِي
98	The Inheritor	*al-Wārith*	الوَارِثُ
99	The Guide to the Right Path	*ar-Rashīd*	الرَّشِيدُ
100	The Patient	*aṣ-Ṣabūr*	الصَّبُورُ

The Merits of Reciting
Sūrat al-Anʿām

It was reported by the Messenger of Allah ﷺ that: "Sūrat al-Anʿām was revealed in its entirety and was carried by seventy thousand angels praising and glorifying Allah. Those who recite this sura will have the gift of these angels asking for mercy and forgiveness for them as many times as the number of verses they recited and for the duration of a complete day and night."

And it has been reported by Ibn ʿAbbās, may Allah be pleased with him, that: "Whoever recites Sūrat al-Anʿām will be of those who are safe on the Day of Judgment and will not be touched by the punishment of the Fire."

Before the Sura

Before reading the sura to address a major concern or difficulty, pray two *raka'āt* after Dhuhr, and then say the following:

Read 11 times

﴿ وَأُفَوِّضُ أَمْرِيٓ إِلَى ٱللَّهِ إِنَّ ٱللَّهَ بَصِيرٌ بِٱلْعِبَادِ ﴾

Wa-ufawwiḍu amrī ila-Allāh; inna-Allāha baṣīrun bil-'ibād.

And I entrust my affairs to Allah; indeed Allah is ever observant of His servants.

Read 11 or 41 times

اَللَّهُمَّ صَلِّ عَلَى سَيِّدِنَا مُحَمَّدٍ وَعَلَى آلِهِ وَصَحْبِهِ وَسَلِّمَ.

Allāhumma ṣalli 'alā sayyidinā Muḥammad wa-'alā ālihi wa-ṣaḥbihi wa-sallim.

O Allah, send your prayers and peace on Prophet Muhammad and his family and companions.

Read 11 or 41 times

أَسْتَغْفِرُ اللَّهَ رَبِّي وَأَتُوبُ إِلَيْهِ.

Astaghfiru-Allāha rabbī wa-atūbu ilayhi.

I seek forgiveness from Allah, my Lord, and I repent to Him.

Read 11 or 41 times

حَسْبُنَا اللّٰهُ وَنِعْمَ الْوَكِيلِ نِعْمَ الْمَوْلَى وَنِعْمَ النَّصِيرِ.

Ḥasbuna-Allāhu wa-ni'mal-wakīl; ni'mal-mawlā wa-ni'man-naṣīr.

Allah is sufficient for us and is the best of all those one can entrust, the best of all allies, and the best of those who provide victory.

Read Sūrat al-Fātiḥa *(The Opening)* 11 or 41 times

﴿ بِسْمِ اللَّهِ الرَّحْمَٰنِ الرَّحِيمِ ۝ الْحَمْدُ لِلَّهِ رَبِّ الْعَالَمِينَ ۝ الرَّحْمَٰنِ الرَّحِيمِ ۝ مَالِكِ يَوْمِ الدِّينِ ۝ إِيَّاكَ نَعْبُدُ وَإِيَّاكَ نَسْتَعِينُ ۝ اهْدِنَا الصِّرَاطَ الْمُسْتَقِيمَ ۝ صِرَاطَ الَّذِينَ أَنْعَمْتَ عَلَيْهِمْ غَيْرِ الْمَغْضُوبِ عَلَيْهِمْ وَلَا الضَّالِّينَ ۝ ﴾

﴿ ① *Bismillāhir Raḥmānir Raḥīm* ② *Alḥamdu li-llāhi rabbil-'ālamīn* ③ *Ar-Raḥmānir Raḥīm* ④ *Māliki yawmid-dīn* ⑤ *Iyyāka na'budu wa-iyyāka nasta'īn* ⑥ *Ihdināṣ-ṣirāṭal-mustaqīm* ⑦ *Ṣirāṭa-lladhīna an'amta 'alayhim ghayril-maghḍūbi 'alayhim wa-lāḍ-ḍāllīn.* ﴾

﴿ ① In the name of Allah, the Merciful, the Compassionate ② All praise is for Allah—Lord of all worlds ③ The Merciful, the Compassionate ④ Master of the Day of Judgment ⑤ You alone we worship and You alone we ask for help ⑥ Guide us along the straight path ⑦ The path of those You have blessed—Not those You are displeased with nor those who are astray. ﴾

Read Sūrat al-Ikhlāṣ *(Sincerity)* 11 or 41 times

بِسْمِ اللَّهِ الرَّحْمَٰنِ الرَّحِيمِ

﴿ قُلْ هُوَ اللَّهُ أَحَدٌ ۝ اللَّهُ الصَّمَدُ ۝ لَمْ يَلِدْ وَلَمْ يُولَدْ ۝ وَلَمْ يَكُن لَّهُ كُفُوًا أَحَدٌ ۝ ﴾

❄ ① *Bismillāhir Raḥmānir Raḥīm* ② *Qul huwa-Allāhu aḥad* ③ *Allāhuṣ-ṣamad* ④ *Lam yalid wa-lam yūlad* ⑤ *Wa-lam yakul-lahu kufuwan aḥad.* ❄

❄ ① Say: He is Allah—One [and Indivisible] ② Allah—the Sustainer needed by all ③ He has never had offspring ④ Nor was He born ⑤ And there is none comparable to Him. ❄

And then read

اَللَّهُمَّ إِنِّي أَسْأَلُكَ بِحَقِّ سُورَةِ الأَنْعَامِ وَبِحَقِّ مُحَمَّدٍ عَلَيْهِ أَفْضَلُ الصَّلَاةِ وَالسَّلَام وَبِحَقِّ أَسْمَائِكَ العِظَامِ أَنْ تَنْظُرَ إِلَيْنَا نَظْرَةَ رَحْمَةٍ وَغُفْرَانٍ وَأَنْ تَحْفَظَنَا مِنْ شَرِّ كُلِّ ذِي شَرٍّ وَمِنْ شَرِّ كُلِّ دَابَّةٍ رَبِّي أَنْتَ آخِذٌ بِنَاصِيَتِهَا إِنَّ رَبِّي عَلَى صِرَاطٍ مُسْتَقِيمٍ اللَّهُمَّ بِحَقِّ حَقِّكَ وَبِحَقِّ النَّبِيِّ.

Allāhumma innī as'aluka bi-ḥaqqi Sūratil-An'ām, wa-bi-ḥaqqi Muḥammadin 'alayhi afḍaluṣ-ṣalāti was-salām, wa-bi-ḥaqqi asmā'ikal-'iẓām, an tanẓura ilaynā naẓrata raḥmatin wa-ghufrān, wa-an taḥfaẓanā min sharri kulli dhī sharr, wa-min sharri kulli dābba, rabbī anta ākhidhun bi-nāṣiyatihā, inna rabbī 'alā ṣirāṭim-mustaqīm. Allāhumma bi-ḥaqqi ḥaqqika wa-bi-ḥaqqin-nabiyy.

O Allah, I ask You by the status of Sūrat al-An'ām and by the status of Prophet Muhammad, upon him be the best of prayers and peace, and by the status of Your greatest names, that You look upon us with a look of mercy and forgiveness, and that You protect us from the evil of everyone who has evil, and from the evil of every moving creature that You hold by its forelock. Indeed my Lord is on a straight path. O Allah, I ask You by the status of Your status and by the status of the Prophet ﷺ.

Then recite the sura.

The Sura

بِسۡمِ ٱللَّهِ ٱلرَّحۡمَٰنِ ٱلرَّحِیمِ

Bismillāhir Raḥmānir Raḥīm

In the name of Allah, the Merciful, the Compassionate

ٱلۡحَمۡدُ لِلَّهِ ٱلَّذِی خَلَقَ ٱلسَّمَٰوَٰتِ وَٱلۡأَرۡضَ وَجَعَلَ ٱلظُّلُمَٰتِ وَٱلنُّورَ ثُمَّ ٱلَّذِینَ كَفَرُواْ بِرَبِّهِمۡ یَعۡدِلُونَ ۝

① *Alḥamdu li-llāhi-lladhī khalaqas-samāwāti wal-arḍa wa-ja'alaẓ-ẓulumāti wan-nūra thumma-lladhīna kafarū bi-rabbihim ya'dilūn.*

① All praise is for Allah who created the heavens and the earth and made darkness and light. Yet the disbelievers set up equals to their Lord [in worship].

هُوَ ٱلَّذِى خَلَقَكُم مِّن طِينٍ ثُمَّ قَضَىٰ أَجَلًا وَأَجَلٌ مُّسَمًّى عِندَهُ ثُمَّ أَنتُمْ تَمْتَرُونَ ۝

② *Huwa-lladhī khalaqakum-min ṭīnin thumma qaḍā ajalan wa-ajalun musamman 'indahu thumma antum tamtarūn.*

② He is the One who created you from clay, then appointed a term [for your death] and another known only to Him [for your resurrection]—yet you continue to doubt!

⸺⬦⸺

وَهُوَ ٱللَّهُ فِى ٱلسَّمَٰوَٰتِ وَفِى ٱلْأَرْضِ يَعْلَمُ سِرَّكُمْ وَجَهْرَكُمْ وَيَعْلَمُ مَا تَكْسِبُونَ ۝

③ *Wa-huwa-Allāhu fis-samāwāti wa-fil-arḍi ya'lamu sirrakum wa-jahrakum wa-ya'lamu mā taksibūn.*

③ He is the Only True God in the heavens and the earth. He knows whatever you conceal and whatever you reveal and knows whatever you do.

⸺⬦⸺

وَمَا تَأْتِيهِم مِّنْ ءَايَةٍ مِّنْ ءَايَٰتِ رَبِّهِمْ إِلَّا كَانُوا۟ عَنْهَا مُعْرِضِينَ ۝

④ *Wa-mā ta'tīhim min āyatim-min āyāti rabbihim illā kānū 'anhā mu'riḍīn.*

④ Whenever a sign comes to them from their Lord, they turn away from it.

⸺⬦⸺

فَقَدْ كَذَّبُواْ بِٱلْحَقِّ لَمَّا جَآءَهُمْ فَسَوْفَ يَأْتِيهِمْ أَنۢبَـٰٓؤُاْ مَا كَانُواْ بِهِۦ يَسْتَهْزِءُونَ ۝

⑤ *Faqad kadhdhabū bil-ḥaqqi lammā jā'ahum fa-sawfa ya'tīhim anbā'u mā kānū bihi yastahzi'ūn.*

⑤ They have indeed rejected the truth when it came to them, so they will soon face the consequences of their ridicule.

أَلَمْ يَرَوْاْ كَمْ أَهْلَكْنَا مِن قَبْلِهِم مِّن قَرْنٍ مَّكَّنَّـٰهُمْ فِى ٱلْأَرْضِ مَا لَمْ نُمَكِّن لَّكُمْ وَأَرْسَلْنَا ٱلسَّمَآءَ عَلَيْهِم مِّدْرَارًا وَجَعَلْنَا ٱلْأَنْهَـٰرَ تَجْرِى مِن تَحْتِهِمْ فَأَهْلَكْنَـٰهُم بِذُنُوبِهِمْ وَأَنشَأْنَا مِنۢ بَعْدِهِمْ قَرْنًا ءَاخَرِينَ ۝

⑥ *Alam yaraw kam ahlaknā min qablihim min qarnin makkannāhum fil-arḍi mā lam numakkil-lakum wa-arsalnas-samā'a 'alayhim midrāran wa-ja'alnal-anhāra tajrī min taḥtihim fa-ahlaknāhum bi-dhunūbihim wa-ansha'nā min ba'dihim qarnan ākharīn.*

⑥ Have they not seen how many [disbelieving] peoples We destroyed before them? We had made them more established in the land than you. We sent down abundant rain for them and made rivers flow at their feet. Then We destroyed them for their sins and replaced them with other peoples.

وَلَوْ نَزَّلْنَا عَلَيْكَ كِتَـٰبًا فِى قِرْطَاسٍ فَلَمَسُوهُ بِأَيْدِيهِمْ لَقَالَ ٱلَّذِينَ كَفَرُوٓا۟ إِنْ هَـٰذَآ إِلَّا سِحْرٌ مُّبِينٌ ۝

⑦ *Wa-law nazzalnā ʿalayka kitāban fī qirṭāsin fa-lamasūhu bi-aydīhim laqāla-lladhīna kafarū in hādhā illā siḥrun mubīn.*

⑦ Had We sent down to you, [O Prophet,] a revelation in writing and they were to touch it with their own hands, the disbelievers would still have said, "This is nothing but pure magic!"

◆━◆

وَقَالُوا۟ لَوْلَآ أُنزِلَ عَلَيْهِ مَلَكٌ ۖ وَلَوْ أَنزَلْنَا مَلَكًا لَّقُضِىَ ٱلْأَمْرُ ثُمَّ لَا يُنظَرُونَ ۝

⑧ *Wa-qālū lawlā unzila ʿalayhi malakun wa-law anzalnā malakan laquḍiyal-amru thumma lā yunẓarūn.*

⑧ They say, "Why has no [visible] angel come with him?" Had We sent down an angel, the matter would have certainly been settled [at once], and they would have never been given more time [to repent].

◆━◆

وَلَوْ جَعَلْنَـٰهُ مَلَكًا لَّجَعَلْنَـٰهُ رَجُلًا وَلَلَبَسْنَا عَلَيْهِم مَّا يَلْبِسُونَ ۝

⑨ *Wa-law jaʿalnāhu malakal-lajaʿalnāhu rajulan wa-lalabasnā ʿalayhim mā yalbisūn.*

⑨ And if We had sent an angel, We would have certainly made it [assume the form of] a man—leaving them more confused than they already are.

وَلَقَدِ ٱسْتُهْزِئَ بِرُسُلٍ مِّن قَبْلِكَ فَحَاقَ بِٱلَّذِينَ سَخِرُواْ مِنْهُم مَّا كَانُواْ بِهِۦ يَسْتَهْزِءُونَ ۝

⑩ *Wa-laqad-istuhzi'a bi-rusulim-min qablika fa-ḥāqa bi-lladhīna sakhirū minhum mā kānū bihi yastahzi'ūn.*

⑩ [Other] messengers had already been ridiculed before you [O Prophet,] but those who mocked them were overtaken by what they used to ridicule.

◆━◆

قُل سِيرُواْ فِي ٱلْأَرْضِ ثُمَّ ٱنظُرُواْ كَيْفَ كَانَ عَٰقِبَةُ ٱلْمُكَذِّبِينَ ۝

⑪ *Qul sīrū fil-arḍi thumma-nẓurū kayfa kāna ʿāqibatul-mukadhdhibīn.*

⑪ Say, "Travel throughout the land and see the fate of the deniers."

◆━◆

قُل لِّمَن مَّا فِي ٱلسَّمَٰوَٰتِ وَٱلْأَرْضِ قُل لِّلَّهِ كَتَبَ عَلَىٰ نَفْسِهِ ٱلرَّحْمَةَ لَيَجْمَعَنَّكُمْ إِلَىٰ يَوْمِ ٱلْقِيَٰمَةِ لَا رَيْبَ فِيهِ ٱلَّذِينَ خَسِرُواْ أَنفُسَهُمْ فَهُمْ لَا يُؤْمِنُونَ ۝

⑫ *Qul limam-mā fis-samāwāti wal-arḍi? Qul li-llāh. Kataba ʿalā nafsihir-raḥma. Layajmaʿannakum ilā yawmil-qiyāmati lā rayba fīh. Alladhīna khasirū anfusahum fahum lā yu'minūn.*

⑫ Ask [them, O Prophet], "To whom belongs everything in the heavens and the earth?" Say, "To Allah!" He has taken upon Himself to be Merciful. He will certainly gather [all of] you together for the Day of Judgment—about which there is no doubt. But those who have ruined themselves will never believe.

٭ وَلَهُۥ مَا سَكَنَ فِى ٱلَّيْلِ وَٱلنَّهَارِ ۚ وَهُوَ ٱلسَّمِيعُ ٱلْعَلِيمُ ﴿١٣﴾

(13) Wa-lahu mā sakana fil-layli wan-nahār. Wa-huwas-samī‘ul-‘alīm.

(13) To Him belongs whatever exists in the day and night. And He is the All-Hearing, All-Knowing.

◆━◆

قُلْ أَغَيْرَ ٱللَّهِ أَتَّخِذُ وَلِيًّا فَاطِرِ ٱلسَّمَـٰوَٰتِ وَٱلْأَرْضِ وَهُوَ يُطْعِمُ وَلَا يُطْعَمُ ۗ قُلْ إِنِّى أُمِرْتُ أَنْ أَكُونَ أَوَّلَ مَنْ أَسْلَمَ ۖ وَلَا تَكُونَنَّ مِنَ ٱلْمُشْرِكِينَ ﴿١٤﴾

(14) Qul aghayra-Allāhi attakhidhu waliyyan fāṭiris-samāwāti wal-arḍi wa-huwa yuṭ‘imu wa-lā yuṭ‘am? Qul innī umirtu an akūna awwala man aslama wa-lā takūnanna minal-mushrikīn.

(14) Say, [O Prophet,] "Will I take any guardian other than Allah, the Originator of the heavens and the earth, who provides for all and is not in need of provision?" Say, "I have been commanded to be the first to submit and not be one of the polytheists."

◆━◆

قُلْ إِنِّى أَخَافُ إِنْ عَصَيْتُ رَبِّى عَذَابَ يَوْمٍ عَظِيمٍ ﴿١٥﴾

(15) Qul innī akhāfu in ‘aṣaytu rabbī ‘adhāba yawmin ‘aẓīm.

(15) Say, "I truly fear—if I were to disobey my Lord—the torment of a tremendous Day."

◆━◆

مَّن يُصْرَفْ عَنْهُ يَوْمَئِذٍ فَقَدْ رَحِمَهُۥ وَذَٰلِكَ ٱلْفَوْزُ ٱلْمُبِينُ ﴿١٦﴾

 *Man yuṣraf ‘anhu yawma’idhin faqad raḥimah. Wa-dhālikal-fawzul-mubīn.*

Whoever is spared the torment of that Day will have certainly been shown Allah's mercy. And that is the absolute triumph.

Pause here and read 41 times

﴿ وَأُفَوِّضُ أَمْرِي إِلَى ٱللَّهِ إِنَّ ٱللَّهَ بَصِيرٌ بِٱلْعِبَادِ ﴾

❖ *Wa-ufawwiḍu amrī ila-Allāh; inna-Allāha baṣīrun bil-‘ibād.* ❖

❖ And I entrust my affairs to Allah; indeed Allah is ever observant of His servants. ❖

وَإِن يَمْسَسْكَ ٱللَّهُ بِضُرٍّ فَلَا كَاشِفَ لَهُۥ إِلَّا هُوَ وَإِن يَمْسَسْكَ بِخَيْرٍ فَهُوَ عَلَىٰ كُلِّ شَيْءٍ قَدِيرٌ ﴿١٧﴾

 *Wa-in yamsaska-Allāhu bi-ḍurrin fa-lā kāshifa lahu illā huw. Wa-in yamsaska bi-khayrin fa-huwa ‘alā kulli shay’in qadīr.*

If Allah touches you with harm, none can undo it except Him. And if He touches you with a blessing, He is Most Capable of everything.

وَهُوَ ٱلْقَاهِرُ فَوْقَ عِبَادِهِۦ ۚ وَهُوَ ٱلْحَكِيمُ ٱلْخَبِيرُ ﴿١٨﴾

(18) *Wa-huwal-qāhiru fawqa ʿibādih. Wa-huwal-ḥakīmul-khabīr.*

(18) He reigns supreme over His creation. And He is the All-Wise, All-Aware.

◆━◆

قُلْ أَىُّ شَىْءٍ أَكْبَرُ شَهَٰدَةً ۖ قُلِ ٱللَّهُ ۖ شَهِيدٌۢ بَيْنِى وَبَيْنَكُمْ ۚ وَأُوحِىَ إِلَىَّ هَٰذَا ٱلْقُرْءَانُ لِأُنذِرَكُم بِهِۦ وَمَنۢ بَلَغَ ۚ أَئِنَّكُمْ لَتَشْهَدُونَ أَنَّ مَعَ ٱللَّهِ ءَالِهَةً أُخْرَىٰ ۚ قُل لَّآ أَشْهَدُ ۚ قُلْ إِنَّمَا هُوَ إِلَٰهٌ وَٰحِدٌ وَإِنَّنِى بَرِىٓءٌ مِّمَّا تُشْرِكُونَ ﴿١٩﴾

(19) *Qul ayyu shay'in akbaru shahāda? Quli-llāh. Shahīdun baynī wa-baynakum. Wa-ūḥiya ilayya hādhal-qur'ānu li-undhirakum bihi wa-man balagh. A-innakum latashhadūna anna maʿa-Allāhi ālihatan ukhrā? Qul lā ashhad. Qul innamā huwa ilāhun wāḥid. Wa-innī barī'un mimmā tushrikūn.*

(19) Ask [them, O Prophet], "Who is the best witness?" Say, "Allah is! He is a Witness between me and you. And this Quran has been revealed to me so that, with it, I may warn you and whoever it reaches. Do you [pagans] testify that there are other gods besides Allah?" [Then] say, "I will never testify [to this]!" [And] say, "There is only One God. And I totally reject whatever [idols] you associate with Him."

◆━◆

ٱلَّذِينَ ءَاتَيْنَـٰهُمُ ٱلْكِتَـٰبَ يَعْرِفُونَهُۥ كَمَا يَعْرِفُونَ أَبْنَآءَهُمُ ٱلَّذِينَ خَسِرُوٓاْ أَنفُسَهُمْ فَهُمْ لَا يُؤْمِنُونَ ﴿٢٠﴾

⟨20⟩ *Alladhīna ātaynāhumul-kitāba ya'rifūnahu kamā ya'rifūna abnā'ahum. Alladhīna khasirū anfusahum fahum lā yu'minūn.*

⟨20⟩ Those to whom We gave the Scripture recognize him [to be a true prophet] as they recognize their own children. Those who have ruined themselves will never believe.

◄►◄►

وَمَنْ أَظْلَمُ مِمَّنِ ٱفْتَرَىٰ عَلَى ٱللَّهِ كَذِبًا أَوْ كَذَّبَ بِـَٔايَـٰتِهِۦٓ إِنَّهُۥ لَا يُفْلِحُ ٱلظَّـٰلِمُونَ ﴿٢١﴾

⟨21⟩ *Wa-man aẓlamu mimman iftarā 'ala-Allāhi kadhiban aw kadhdhaba bi-āyātih? Innahu lā yufliḥuẓ-ẓālimūn.*

⟨21⟩ Who does more wrong than those who fabricate lies against Allah or deny His signs? Indeed, the wrongdoers will never succeed.

◄►◄►

وَيَوْمَ نَحْشُرُهُمْ جَمِيعًا ثُمَّ نَقُولُ لِلَّذِينَ أَشْرَكُوٓاْ أَيْنَ شُرَكَآؤُكُمُ ٱلَّذِينَ كُنتُمْ تَزْعُمُونَ ﴿٢٢﴾

⟨22⟩ *Wa-yawma naḥshuruhum jamī'an thumma naqūlu li-lladhīna ashrakū: ayna shurakā'ukumu-lladhīna kuntum taz'umūn?*

⟨22⟩ [Consider] the Day We will gather them all together then ask those who associated others with [with Allah in worship] "Where are those gods you used to claim?"

ثُمَّ لَمْ تَكُن فِتْنَتُهُمْ إِلَّا أَن قَالُواْ وَٱللَّهِ رَبِّنَا مَا كُنَّا مُشْرِكِينَ ۝

(23) *Thumma lam takun fitnatuhum illā an qālū: wa-Allāhi rabbinā mā kunnā mushrikīn.*

(23) Their only argument will be: "By Allah, our Lord! We were never polytheists."

⸺◆⸺

ٱنظُرْ كَيْفَ كَذَبُواْ عَلَىٰٓ أَنفُسِهِمْ وَضَلَّ عَنْهُم مَّا كَانُواْ يَفْتَرُونَ ۝

(24) *Unẓur kayfa kadhabū ʿalā anfusihim, wa-ḍalla ʿanhum mā kānū yaftarūn.*

(24) See how they will lie about themselves and how those [gods] they fabricated will fail them!

⸺◆⸺

وَمِنْهُم مَّن يَسْتَمِعُ إِلَيْكَ وَجَعَلْنَا عَلَىٰ قُلُوبِهِمْ أَكِنَّةً أَن يَفْقَهُوهُ وَفِىٓ ءَاذَانِهِمْ وَقْرًا وَإِن يَرَوْاْ كُلَّ ءَايَةٍ لَّا يُؤْمِنُواْ بِهَا حَتَّىٰٓ إِذَا جَآءُوكَ يُجَٰدِلُونَكَ يَقُولُ ٱلَّذِينَ كَفَرُوٓاْ إِنْ هَٰذَآ إِلَّآ أَسَٰطِيرُ ٱلْأَوَّلِينَ ۝

(25) *Wa-minhum man yastamiʿu ilayka, wa-jaʿalnā ʿalā qulūbihim akinnatan an yafqahūhu wa-fī ādhānihim waqra; wa-in yaraw kulla āyatin lā yu'minū bihā, ḥattā idhā jā'ūka yujādilūnaka yaqūlu-lladhīna kafarū in hādhā illā asāṭīrul-awwalīn.*

(25) There are some of them who [pretend to] listen to your recitation [of the Quran], but We have cast veils over their hearts—leaving them unable to comprehend it—and deafness in their ears. Even if they were to see every sign, they still would not believe in them. The disbelievers would [even] come to argue with you, saying, "This [Quran] is nothing but ancient fables!"

وَهُمْ يَنْهَوْنَ عَنْهُ وَيَنْـَٔوْنَ عَنْهُ ۖ وَإِن يُهْلِكُونَ إِلَّآ أَنفُسَهُمْ وَمَا يَشْعُرُونَ ۝

26 *Wa-hum yanhawna ʿanhu wa-yanʾawna ʿanh; wa-in yuhlikūna illā anfusahum wa-mā yashʿurūn.*

26 They turn others away from the Prophet and distance themselves as well. They ruin none but themselves, yet they fail to perceive it.

وَلَوْ تَرَىٰٓ إِذْ وُقِفُوا۟ عَلَى ٱلنَّارِ فَقَالُوا۟ يَـٰلَيْتَنَا نُرَدُّ وَلَا نُكَذِّبَ بِـَٔايَـٰتِ رَبِّنَا وَنَكُونَ مِنَ ٱلْمُؤْمِنِينَ ۝

27 *Wa-law tarā idh wuqifū ʿalan-nār, fa-qālū: yā laytanā nuraddu wa-lā nukadhdhiba bi-āyāti rabbinā wa-nakūna minal-muʾminīn.*

27 If only you could see when they will be detained before the Fire! They will cry, "Oh! If only we could be sent back, we would never deny the signs of our Lord and we would [surely] be of the believers."

بَلْ بَدَا لَهُم مَّا كَانُوا۟ يُخْفُونَ مِن قَبْلُ ۖ وَلَوْ رُدُّوا۟ لَعَادُوا۟ لِمَا نُهُوا۟ عَنْهُ وَإِنَّهُمْ لَكَـٰذِبُونَ ۝

28 *Bal badā lahum mā kānū yukhfūna min qabl; wa-law ruddū la-ʿādū limā nuhū ʿanhu wa-innahum lakādhibūn.*

28 But no! [They only say this] because the truth they used to hide will become all too clear to them. Even if they were to be sent back, they would certainly revert to what they were forbidden. Indeed they are liars!

وَقَالُوٓاْ إِنْ هِىَ إِلَّا حَيَاتُنَا ٱلدُّنْيَا وَمَا نَحْنُ بِمَبْعُوثِينَ ﴿٢٩﴾

(29) *Wa-qālū: in hiya illā ḥayātunad-dunyā wa-mā naḥnu bi-mabʿūthīn.*

(29) They insisted, "There is nothing beyond this worldly life and we will never be resurrected."

❖

وَلَوْ تَرَىٰٓ إِذْ وُقِفُواْ عَلَىٰ رَبِّهِمْ قَالَ أَلَيْسَ هَٰذَا بِٱلْحَقِّ قَالُواْ بَلَىٰ وَرَبِّنَا قَالَ فَذُوقُواْ ٱلْعَذَابَ بِمَا كُنتُمْ تَكْفُرُونَ ﴿٣٠﴾

(30) *Wa-law tarā idh wuqifū ʿalā rabbihim; qāla: alaysa hādhā bil-ḥaqq? Qālū: balā wa-rabbinā. Qāla: fa-dhūqul-ʿadhāba bimā kuntum takfurūn.*

(30) But if only you could see when they will be detained before their Lord! He will ask [them], "Is this [Hereafter] not the truth?" They will cry, "Absolutely, by our Lord!" He will say, "Then taste the punishment for your disbelief."

❖

قَدْ خَسِرَ ٱلَّذِينَ كَذَّبُواْ بِلِقَآءِ ٱللَّهِ حَتَّىٰٓ إِذَا جَآءَتْهُمُ ٱلسَّاعَةُ بَغْتَةً قَالُواْ يَٰحَسْرَتَنَا عَلَىٰ مَا فَرَّطْنَا فِيهَا وَهُمْ يَحْمِلُونَ أَوْزَارَهُمْ عَلَىٰ ظُهُورِهِمْ أَلَا سَآءَ مَا يَزِرُونَ ﴿٣١﴾

(31) *Qad khasira-lladhīna kadhdhabū bi-liqāʾi-llāh; ḥattā idhā jāʾat-humus-sāʿatu baghtatan qālū yā ḥasratanā ʿalā mā farraṭnā fī-hā wa-hum yaḥmilūna awzāra-hum ʿalā ẓuhūrihim; alā sāʾa mā yazirūn.*

(31) Losers indeed are those who deny the meeting with Allah until the Hour takes them by surprise, then they will cry, "Woe to us for having ignored this!" They will bear [the burden of] their sins on their backs. Evil indeed is their burden!

وَمَا ٱلْحَيَوٰةُ ٱلدُّنْيَآ إِلَّا لَعِبٌ وَلَهْوٌ وَلَلدَّارُ ٱلْءَاخِرَةُ خَيْرٌ لِّلَّذِينَ يَتَّقُونَ أَفَلَا تَعْقِلُونَ ۞

(32) *Wa-mal-ḥayātud-dunyā illā laʿibun wa-lahw; wa-lad-dārul-ākhiratu khayrul-li-lladhīna yattaqūn; afalā taʿqilūn.*

(32) This worldly life is no more than play and amusement, but far better is the [eternal] Home of the Hereafter for those mindful of Allah. Will you not then understand?

◆━◆

قَدْ نَعْلَمُ إِنَّهُۥ لَيَحْزُنُكَ ٱلَّذِى يَقُولُونَ فَإِنَّهُمْ لَا يُكَذِّبُونَكَ وَلَٰكِنَّ ٱلظَّٰلِمِينَ بِـَٔايَٰتِ ٱللَّهِ يَجْحَدُونَ ۞

(33) *Qad naʿlamu innahu la-yaḥzunuka-lladhī yaqūlūn; fa-innahum lā yukadhibūnaka wa-lākinnaẓ-ẓālimīna bi-āyāti-llāhi yajḥadūn.*

(33) We certainly know that what they say grieves you [O Prophet]. It is not your honesty they question—it is Allah's signs that the wrongdoers deny.

◆━◆

وَلَقَدْ كُذِّبَتْ رُسُلٌ مِّن قَبْلِكَ فَصَبَرُواْ عَلَىٰ مَا كُذِّبُواْ وَأُوذُواْ حَتَّىٰٓ أَتَىٰهُمْ نَصْرُنَا وَلَا مُبَدِّلَ لِكَلِمَٰتِ ٱللَّهِ وَلَقَدْ جَآءَكَ مِن نَّبَإِى۟ ٱلْمُرْسَلِينَ ۞

(34) *Wa-laqad kudhdhibat rusulun min qablika fa-ṣabarū ʿalā mā kudhdhibū wa-ūdhū ḥattā atā-hum naṣrunā; wa-lā mubaddila li-kalimāti-llāh; wa-la-qad jāʾaka min nabaʾil-mursalīn.*

(34) Indeed, messengers before you were rejected but patiently endured rejection and persecution until Our help came to them. And Allah's promise [to help] is never broken. And you have already received some of the narratives of these messengers.

وَإِن كَانَ كَبُرَ عَلَيْكَ إِعْرَاضُهُمْ فَإِنِ ٱسْتَطَعْتَ أَن تَبْتَغِىَ نَفَقًا فِى ٱلْأَرْضِ أَوْ سُلَّمًا فِى ٱلسَّمَاءِ فَتَأْتِيَهُم بِـَٔايَةٍ وَلَوْ شَآءَ ٱللَّهُ لَجَمَعَهُمْ عَلَى ٱلْهُدَىٰ فَلَا تَكُونَنَّ مِنَ ٱلْجَٰهِلِينَ ۝

³⁵ *Wa-in kāna kabura ‘alayka i‘rāḍuhum fa-ini-staṭa‘ta an tabtaghiya nafaqan fil-arḍi aw sullaman fis-samā’i fa-ta’tiya-hum bi-āyatin; wa-law shā’a Allāhu la-jama‘a-hum ‘alal-hudā; fa-lā takūnanna minal-jāhilīn.*

³⁵ If you find their denial unbearable, then build—if you can—a tunnel through the earth or stairs to the sky to bring them a [more compelling] sign. Had Allah so willed, He could have guided them all. So do not be one of those ignorant [of this fact].

* * *

﴿ إِنَّمَا يَسْتَجِيبُ ٱلَّذِينَ يَسْمَعُونَ وَٱلْمَوْتَىٰ يَبْعَثُهُمُ ٱللَّهُ ثُمَّ إِلَيْهِ يُرْجَعُونَ ۝

³⁶ *Innamā yastajību-lladhīna yasma‘ūn; wal-mawtā yab‘athu-humu-llāhu thumma ilayhi yurja‘ūn.*

³⁶ Only the attentive will respond [to your call]. As for the dead, Allah will raise them up, then to Him they will [all] be returned.

* * *

وَقَالُواْ لَوْلَا نُزِّلَ عَلَيْهِ ءَايَةٌ مِّن رَّبِّهِۦ قُلْ إِنَّ ٱللَّهَ قَادِرٌ عَلَىٰٓ أَن يُنَزِّلَ ءَايَةً وَلَٰكِنَّ أَكْثَرَهُمْ لَا يَعْلَمُونَ ۝

(37) *Wa-qālū: law-lā nuzzila ʿalayhi āyatun min rabbih. Qul: inna-Allāha qādirun ʿalā an yunazzila āyatan wa-lākinna aktharahum lā yaʿlamūn.*

(37) They ask, "Why has no [other] sign been sent down to him from his Lord?" Say, [O Prophet,] "Allah certainly has the power to send down a sign"—though most of them do not know.

وَمَا مِن دَآبَّةٍ فِى ٱلْأَرْضِ وَلَا طَٰٓئِرٍ يَطِيرُ بِجَنَاحَيْهِ إِلَّآ أُمَمٌ أَمْثَالُكُم مَّا فَرَّطْنَا فِى ٱلْكِتَٰبِ مِن شَىْءٍ ثُمَّ إِلَىٰ رَبِّهِمْ يُحْشَرُونَ ۝

(38) *Wa-mā min dābbatin fil-arḍi wa-lā ṭāʾirin yaṭīru bi-janāḥayhi illā umamun amthālukum; mā farraṭnā fil-kitābi min shayʾin thumma ilā rabbihim yuḥsharūn.*

(38) All living beings roaming the earth and winged birds soaring in the sky are communities like yourselves. We have left nothing out of the Record. Then to their Lord they will be gathered all together.

وَٱلَّذِينَ كَذَّبُواْ بِـَٔايَٰتِنَا صُمٌّ وَبُكْمٌ فِى ٱلظُّلُمَٰتِ مَن يَشَإِ ٱللَّهُ يُضْلِلْهُ وَمَن يَشَأْ يَجْعَلْهُ عَلَىٰ صِرَٰطٍ مُّسْتَقِيمٍ ۝

(39) *Wa-lladhīna kadhdhabū bi-āyātinā ṣummun wa-bukmun fiẓ-ẓulumāt; man yashāʾi-llāhu yuḍlilhu wa-man yashāʾ yajʿalhu ʿalā ṣirāṭim-mustaqīm.*

(39) Those who deny Our signs are [willfully] deaf and dumb—lost in darkness. Allah leaves whoever He wills to stray and guides whoever He wills to the Straight Way.

Pause here and read 41 times

﴿ وَأُفَوِّضُ أَمْرِى إِلَى ٱللَّهِ إِنَّ ٱللَّهَ بَصِيرٌۢ بِٱلْعِبَادِ ﴾

﴿ *Wa-ufawwiḍu amrī ila-Allāh; inna-*
Allāha baṣīrun bil-ʿibād. ﴾

﴿ And I entrust my affairs to Allah; indeed
Allah is ever observant of His servants. ﴾

قُلْ أَرَءَيْتَكُمْ إِنْ أَتَىٰكُمْ عَذَابُ ٱللَّهِ أَوْ أَتَتْكُمُ ٱلسَّاعَةُ أَغَيْرَ ٱللَّهِ
تَدْعُونَ إِن كُنتُمْ صَٰدِقِينَ ⓴

⑩ *Qul: araʾaytum in atākum ʿadhābu-llāhi aw atatkum as-sāʿatu*
a-ghayra-Allāhi tadʿūna in kuntum ṣādiqīn.

⑩ Ask [them, O Prophet], "Imagine if you were overwhelmed by
Allah's torment or the Hour—would you call upon any other than
Allah [for help]? [Answer me] if your claims are true!

بَلْ إِيَّاهُ تَدْعُونَ فَيَكْشِفُ مَا تَدْعُونَ إِلَيْهِ إِن شَآءَ وَتَنسَوْنَ مَا
تُشْرِكُونَ ㉔

㊶ *Bal iyyāhu tadʿūna fa-yakshifu mā tadʿūna ilayhi in shāʾa wa-*
tansawna mā tushrikūn.

㊶ No! He is the only One you would call. And if He willed, He
could remove the affliction that made you invoke Him. Only then
will you forget whatever you associate with Him [in worship]."

وَلَقَدْ أَرْسَلْنَا إِلَىٰ أُمَمٍ مِّن قَبْلِكَ فَأَخَذْنَاهُم بِٱلْبَأْسَآءِ وَٱلضَّرَّآءِ لَعَلَّهُمْ يَتَضَرَّعُونَ ﴿٤٢﴾

⁴² *Wa-la-qad arsalnā ilā umamim-min qablika fa-akhadhnā-hum bil-ba'sā'i waḍ-ḍarrā'i la'allahum yataḍarra'ūn.*

⁴² Indeed, We have sent messengers before you, [O Prophet,] to other people who We put through suffering and adversity [for their denial], so perhaps they would be humbled.

◆—◆

فَلَوْلَآ إِذْ جَآءَهُم بَأْسُنَا تَضَرَّعُواْ وَلَٰكِن قَسَتْ قُلُوبُهُمْ وَزَيَّنَ لَهُمُ ٱلشَّيْطَٰنُ مَا كَانُواْ يَعْمَلُونَ ﴿٤٣﴾

⁴³ *Fa-lawlā idh jā'ahum ba'sunā taḍarra'ū wa-lākin qasat qulūbuhum wa-zayyana lahumush-shayṭānu mā kānū ya'malūn.*

⁴³ Why did they not humble themselves when We made them suffer? Instead, their hearts were hardened, and Satan made their misdeeds appealing to them.

◆—◆

فَلَمَّا نَسُواْ مَا ذُكِّرُواْ بِهِۦ فَتَحْنَا عَلَيْهِمْ أَبْوَٰبَ كُلِّ شَىْءٍ حَتَّىٰٓ إِذَا فَرِحُواْ بِمَآ أُوتُوٓاْ أَخَذْنَٰهُم بَغْتَةً فَإِذَا هُم مُّبْلِسُونَ ﴿٤٤﴾

⁴⁴ *Fa-lammā nasū mā dhukkirū bihi fataḥnā 'alayhim abwāba kulli shay'in ḥattā idhā fariḥū bimā ūtu, akhadhnāhum baghtatan fa-idhā hum mublisūn.*

⁴⁴ When they became oblivious to warnings, We showered them with everything they desired. But just as they became prideful of what they were given, We seized them by surprise, then they instantly fell into despair!

فَقُطِعَ دَابِرُ ٱلْقَوْمِ ٱلَّذِينَ ظَلَمُواْ وَٱلْحَمْدُ لِلَّهِ رَبِّ ٱلْعَٰلَمِينَ ﴿٤٥﴾

(45) *Fa-quṭiʿa dābirul-qawmi-lladhīna ẓalamū wal-ḥamdu li-llāhi rabbil-ʿālamīn.*

(45) So the wrongdoers were utterly uprooted. And all praise is for Allah—Lord of all worlds.

قُلْ أَرَءَيْتُمْ إِنْ أَخَذَ ٱللَّهُ سَمْعَكُمْ وَأَبْصَٰرَكُمْ وَخَتَمَ عَلَىٰ قُلُوبِكُم مَّنْ إِلَٰهٌ غَيْرُ ٱللَّهِ يَأْتِيكُم بِهِ ٱنظُرْ كَيْفَ نُصَرِّفُ ٱلْأَيَٰتِ ثُمَّ هُمْ يَصْدِفُونَ ﴿٤٦﴾

(46) *Qul: arāʾaytum in akhadha-Allāhu samʿakum wa-abṣārakum wa-khatama ʿalā qulūbikum man ilāhun ghayru-llāhi yaʾtīkum bih. Unẓur kayfa nuṣarriful-āyāti thumma hum yaṣdifūn.*

(46) Ask [them, O Prophet], "Imagine if Allah were to take away your hearing or sight, or seal your hearts—who else other than Allah could restore it?" See [O Prophet] how We vary the signs, yet they still turn away.

قُلْ أَرَءَيْتَكُمْ إِنْ أَتَىٰكُمْ عَذَابُ ٱللَّهِ بَغْتَةً أَوْ جَهْرَةً هَلْ يُهْلَكُ إِلَّا ٱلْقَوْمُ ٱلظَّٰلِمُونَ ﴿٤٧﴾

(47) *Qul: arāʾaytakum in atākum ʿadhābu-llāhi baghtatan aw jahratan hal yuhlaku illal-qawmuẓ-ẓālimūn.*

(47) Ask, "Imagine if Allah's punishment were to overwhelm you with or without warning—who would be destroyed other than the wrongdoers?"

وَمَا نُرْسِلُ ٱلْمُرْسَلِينَ إِلَّا مُبَشِّرِينَ وَمُنذِرِينَ ۖ فَمَنْ ءَامَنَ وَأَصْلَحَ فَلَا خَوْفٌ عَلَيْهِمْ وَلَا هُمْ يَحْزَنُونَ ﴿٤٨﴾

(48) *Wa-mā nursilul-mursalīna illā mubashshirīna wa-mundhirīn; fa-man āmana wa-aṣlaḥa fa-lā khawfun ʿalayhim wa-lā hum yaḥzanūn.*

(48) We have sent messengers only as deliverers of good news and as warners. Whoever believes and does good, there will be no fear for them, nor will they grieve.

◆━◆━◆

وَٱلَّذِينَ كَذَّبُواْ بِـَٔايَٰتِنَا يَمَسُّهُمُ ٱلْعَذَابُ بِمَا كَانُواْ يَفْسُقُونَ ﴿٤٩﴾

(49) *Wa-lladhīna kadhdhabū bi-āyātinā yamassuhumul-ʿadhābu bimā kānū yafsuqūn.*

(49) But those who deny Our signs will be afflicted with punishment for their rebelliousness.

◆━◆━◆

قُل لَّآ أَقُولُ لَكُمْ عِندِى خَزَآئِنُ ٱللَّهِ وَلَآ أَعْلَمُ ٱلْغَيْبَ وَلَآ أَقُولُ لَكُمْ إِنِّى مَلَكٌ ۖ إِنْ أَتَّبِعُ إِلَّا مَا يُوحَىٰ إِلَىَّ قُلْ هَلْ يَسْتَوِى ٱلْأَعْمَىٰ وَٱلْبَصِيرُ أَفَلَا تَتَفَكَّرُونَ ﴿٥٠﴾

(50) *Qul: lā aqūlu lakum ʿindī khazāʾinu-llāhi wa-lā aʿlamul-ghayba wa-lā aqūlu lakum innī malak; in attabiʿu illā mā yūḥā ilayy. Qul: hal yastawil-aʿmā wal-baṣīr. Afalā tatafakkarūn.*

(50) Say, [O Prophet], "I do not say to you that I possess Allah's treasuries or know the unseen, nor do I claim to be an angel. I only follow what is revealed to me." Say, "Are those blind [to the truth] equal to those who can see? Will you not then reflect?"

وَأَنذِرْ بِهِ ٱلَّذِينَ يَخَافُونَ أَن يُحْشَرُوٓاْ إِلَىٰ رَبِّهِمْ لَيْسَ لَهُم مِّن دُونِهِۦ
وَلِيٌّ وَلَا شَفِيعٌ لَّعَلَّهُمْ يَتَّقُونَ ۝

⑤ *Wa-andhir bihi-lladhīna yakhāfūna an yuḥsharū ilā rabbihim laysa
lahum min dūnihi walīyyun walā shafiʿul-laʿallahum yattaqūn.*

⑤ Warn with this [Quran] those who are awed by the prospect
of being gathered before their Lord—when they will have no
protector or intercessor besides Him—so perhaps they will be
mindful [of Him].

◆—◆

وَلَا تَطْرُدِ ٱلَّذِينَ يَدْعُونَ رَبَّهُم بِٱلْغَدَوٰةِ وَٱلْعَشِيِّ يُرِيدُونَ وَجْهَهُۥ مَا
عَلَيْكَ مِنْ حِسَابِهِم مِّن شَىْءٍ وَمَا مِنْ حِسَابِكَ عَلَيْهِم مِّن شَىْءٍ
فَتَطْرُدَهُمْ فَتَكُونَ مِنَ ٱلظَّٰلِمِينَ ۝

⑤ *Wa-lā taṭrudi-lladhīna yadʿūna rabbahum bil-ghadāti wal-ʿashiyyi
yurīdūna wajhahu mā ʿalayka min ḥisābihim min shayʾin wa-mā min
ḥisābika ʿalayhim min shayʾin fa-taṭrudahum fa-takūna minaẓ-ẓālimīn.*

⑤ [O Prophet!] Do not dismiss those [poor believers] who invoke
their Lord morning and evening, seeking His pleasure. You are not
accountable for them whatsoever, nor are they accountable for
you. So do not dismiss them, or you will be one of the wrongdoers.

◆—◼—◆

وَكَذَٰلِكَ فَتَنَّا بَعْضَهُم بِبَعْضٍ لِّيَقُولُوٓا أَهَـٰٓؤُلَآءِ مَنَّ ٱللَّهُ عَلَيْهِم مِّنۢ بَيْنِنَآ أَلَيْسَ ٱللَّهُ بِأَعْلَمَ بِٱلشَّـٰكِرِينَ ۝

(53) *Wa-kadhālika fatannā baʿḍahum bi-baʿḍil-li-yaqūlū a-hāʾulāʾi manna-llāhu ʿalayhim min bayninā? A-laysa-Allāhu bi-aʿlama bish-shākirīn.*

(53) In this way We have tested some by means of others, so those [disbelievers] may say, "Has Allah favored these [poor believers] out of all of us?" Does Allah not best recognize the grateful?

وَإِذَا جَآءَكَ ٱلَّذِينَ يُؤْمِنُونَ بِـَٔايَـٰتِنَا فَقُلْ سَلَـٰمٌ عَلَيْكُمْ كَتَبَ رَبُّكُمْ عَلَىٰ نَفْسِهِ ٱلرَّحْمَةَ أَنَّهُۥ مَنْ عَمِلَ مِنكُمْ سُوٓءًۢا بِجَهَـٰلَةٍ ثُمَّ تَابَ مِنۢ بَعْدِهِۦ وَأَصْلَحَ فَأَنَّهُۥ غَفُورٌ رَّحِيمٌ ۝

(54) *Wa-idhā jāʾaka-lladhīna yuʾminūna bi-āyātinā fa-qul salāmun ʿalaykum kataba rabbukum ʿalā nafsihir-raḥmata annahu man ʿamila minkum sūʾan bi-jahālatin thumma tāba min baʿdihi wa-aṣlaḥa fa-annahu ghafūrur-raḥīm.*

(54) When the believers in Our revelations come to you, say, "Peace be upon you! Your Lord has taken upon Himself to be Merciful. Whoever among you commits evil ignorantly [or recklessly], then repents afterwards and mends their ways, then Allah is truly All-Forgiving, Most Merciful."

وَكَذَٰلِكَ نُفَصِّلُ ٱلْأَيَٰتِ وَلِتَسْتَبِينَ سَبِيلُ ٱلْمُجْرِمِينَ ۝

(55) *Wa-kadhālika nufaṣṣilul-ayāti wa-li-tastabīna sabīlul-mujrimīn.*

(55) This is how We make Our signs clear, so the way of the wicked may become distinct.

◆━◆

قُلْ إِنِّي نُهِيتُ أَنْ أَعْبُدَ ٱلَّذِينَ تَدْعُونَ مِن دُونِ ٱللَّهِ قُل لَّآ أَتَّبِعُ أَهْوَآءَكُمْ قَدْ ضَلَلْتُ إِذًا وَمَآ أَنَا۠ مِنَ ٱلْمُهْتَدِينَ ۝

(56) *Qul innī nuhītu an a‘buda-lladhīna tad‘ūna min dūni-llāhi qul lā attabi‘u ahwā’akum qad ḍalaltu idhan wa-mā anā minal-muhtadīn.*

(56) Say, [O Prophet,] "I have been forbidden to worship those you invoke besides Allah." Say, "I will not follow your desires, for I then would certainly be astray and not one of those [rightly] guided."

◆━◆

قُلْ إِنِّي عَلَىٰ بَيِّنَةٍ مِّن رَّبِّي وَكَذَّبْتُم بِهِۦ مَا عِندِي مَا تَسْتَعْجِلُونَ بِهِۦٓ إِنِ ٱلْحُكْمُ إِلَّا لِلَّهِ يَقُصُّ ٱلْحَقَّ وَهُوَ خَيْرُ ٱلْفَٰصِلِينَ ۝

(57) *Qul innī ‘alā bayyinatin mir-rabbī wa-kadhdhabtum bihi mā ‘indī mā tasta‘jilūna bihi inil-ḥukmu illā li-llāhi yaquṣṣul-ḥaqqa wa-huwa khayrul-fāṣilīn.*

(57) Say, [O Prophet,] "Indeed, I stand on a clear proof from my Lord—yet you have denied it. That [torment] you seek to hasten is not within my power. It is only Allah who decides [its time]. He declares the truth. And He is the Best of Judges."

قُل لَّوۡ أَنَّ عِندِى مَا تَسۡتَعۡجِلُونَ بِهِۦ لَقُضِىَ ٱلۡأَمۡرُ بَيۡنِى وَبَيۡنَكُمۡۗ وَٱللَّهُ أَعۡلَمُ بِٱلظَّـٰلِمِينَ ٥٨

(58) *Qul law anna ʿindī mā tastaʿjilūna bihi la-quḍiyal-amru baynī wa-baynakum wa-Allāhu aʿlamu biẓ-ẓālimīn.*

(58) Say [also], "If what you seek to hasten were within my power, the matter between us would have already been settled. But Allah knows the wrongdoers best."

◆—◀▬▶—◆

* وَعِندَهُۥ مَفَاتِحُ ٱلۡغَيۡبِ لَا يَعۡلَمُهَآ إِلَّا هُوَۚ وَيَعۡلَمُ مَا فِى ٱلۡبَرِّ وَٱلۡبَحۡرِۚ وَمَا تَسۡقُطُ مِن وَرَقَةٍ إِلَّا يَعۡلَمُهَا وَلَا حَبَّةٍ فِى ظُلُمَـٰتِ ٱلۡأَرۡضِ وَلَا رَطۡبٍ وَلَا يَابِسٍ إِلَّا فِى كِتَـٰبٍ مُّبِينٍ ٥٩

(59) *Wa-ʿindahu mafātiḥul-ghaybi lā yaʿlamuhā illā huwa wa-yaʿlamu mā fil-barri wal-baḥri wa-mā tasquṭu min waraqatin illā yaʿlamuhā wa-lā ḥabbatin fī ẓulumātil-arḍi wa-lā raṭbin wa-lā yābisin illā fī kitābin mubīn.*

(59) With Him are the keys of the unseen—no one knows them except Him. And He knows what is in the land and sea. Not even a leaf falls without His knowledge, nor a grain in the darkness of the earth or anything—green or dry—but is [written] in a perfect Record.

◆—◀▬▶—◆

Pause here and read

اللَّهُمَّ إِنِّي أَسْأَلُكَ بِاسْمِكَ الْمَكْنُونِ الْمَخْزُونِ الطُّهْرِ الطَّاهِرِ الْمُبَارَك وَ أَسْأَلُكَ بِاسْمِكَ الْعَظِيمِ وَ سُلْطَانِكَ الْقَدِيمِ يَا وَاهِبَ الْعَطَايَا يَا مُطْلِقَ الْأَسَارَى يَا فَكَّاكَ الرِّقَابِ مِنَ النَّارِ أَسْأَلُكَ أَنْ تُصَلّي عَلَى سَيِّدِنَا مُحَمَّدٍ وَآلِ سَيِّدِنَا مُحَمَّدٍ وَتُعْتِقَ رِقَابَنَا مِنَ النَّارِ وَأَنْ تُخْرِجَنا مِنَ الدُّنيَا سَالِمِينَ وَتُدْخِلَنَا الجَنَّةَ آمِنِينَ وَأَنْ تَجْعَلَ يَومَنا أَوَّلَهُ صَلاحاً وَأَوْسَطَهُ نَجَاحاً وَآخِرَهُ فَلَاحاً إِنَّكَ عَلَى كُلِّ شيءٍ قَدِير.

*Allāhumma innī as'aluka bismikal-maknūnil-makhzūniṭ-ṭuhriṭ-
ṭāhiril-mubārak, wa-as'aluka bismikal-'aẓīmi wa-sulṭānikal-qadīm,
yā wāhibal-'aṭāyā, yā muṭliqal-asārā, yā fakkākar-riqābi minan-
nār, as'aluka an tuṣallī 'alā sayyidinā Muḥammad wa-āli sayyidinā
Muḥammad wa-tu'tiqa riqābanā minan-nār, wa-an tukhrijanā
minad-dunyā sālimīn, wa-tudkhilanal-jannata āminīn, wa-an taj'ala
yawmanā awwalahu ṣalāḥa, wa-awsaṭahu najāḥa, wa-ākhirahu falāḥa,
innaka 'alā kulli shay'in qadīr.*

O Allah, I ask You by the status of Your treasured, hidden, pure,
purifying, blessed name, and I ask You by your great name and by
Your eternal dominion, O Bestower of gifts, O Liberator of captives,
O You who frees souls from the Hellfire, to send Your prayers upon
Prophet Muhammad and the family of Prophet Muhammad. Save
us from the Hellfire, bring us out of this world safe, enter us into
Heaven secure. Make our day begin with goodness, give us success
at its midpoint, and end it with prosperity. Indeed You hold power
over all things.

وَهُوَ ٱلَّذِى يَتَوَفَّىٰكُم بِٱلَّيْلِ وَيَعْلَمُ مَا جَرَحْتُم بِٱلنَّهَارِ ثُمَّ يَبْعَثُكُمْ فِيهِ لِيُقْضَىٰٓ أَجَلٌ مُّسَمًّى ثُمَّ إِلَيْهِ مَرْجِعُكُمْ ثُمَّ يُنَبِّئُكُم بِمَا كُنتُمْ تَعْمَلُونَ ۝

(60) *Wa-huwa-lladhī yatawaffākum bil-layli wa-ya'lamu mā jaraḥtum bin-nahāri thumma yab'athukum fīhi li-yuqḍā ajalun musamman thumma ilayhi marji'ukum thumma yunabbi'ukum bimā kuntum ta'malūn.*

(60) He is the One who calls back your souls by night and knows what you do by day, then revives you daily to complete your appointed term. To Him is your [ultimate] return, then He will inform you of what you used to do.

وَهُوَ ٱلْقَاهِرُ فَوْقَ عِبَادِهِ وَيُرْسِلُ عَلَيْكُمْ حَفَظَةً حَتَّىٰٓ إِذَا جَآءَ أَحَدَكُمُ ٱلْمَوْتُ تَوَفَّتْهُ رُسُلُنَا وَهُمْ لَا يُفَرِّطُونَ ۝

(61) *Wa-huwal-qāhiru fawqa 'ibādihi wa-yursilu 'alaykum ḥafaẓatan ḥattā idhā jā'a aḥadakumul-mawtu tawaffathu rusulunā wa-hum lā yufarriṭūn.*

(61) He reigns supreme over all of His creation and sends recording angels, watching over you. When death comes to any of you, Our angels take their soul, never neglecting this duty.

ثُمَّ رُدُّوٓاْ إِلَى ٱللَّهِ مَوْلَىٰهُمُ ٱلْحَقِّ أَلَا لَهُ ٱلْحُكْمُ وَهُوَ أَسْرَعُ ٱلْحَـٰسِبِينَ ۝

(62) *Thumma ruddū ila-llāhi mawlāhumul-ḥaqq; alā lahul-ḥukmu wa-huwa asra'ul-ḥāsibīn.*

(62) Then they are [all] returned to Allah—their True Master. Judgment is His [alone]. And He is the Swiftest Reckoner.

◆━◆

قُلْ مَن يُنَجِّيكُم مِّن ظُلُمَـٰتِ ٱلْبَرِّ وَٱلْبَحْرِ تَدْعُونَهُۥ تَضَرُّعًا وَخُفْيَةً لَّئِنْ أَنجَـٰنَا مِنْ هَـٰذِهِۦ لَنَكُونَنَّ مِنَ ٱلشَّـٰكِرِينَ ۝

(63) *Qul man yunajjīkum min ẓulumātil-barri wal-baḥri tad'ūnahu taḍarru'an wa-khufyatan la-in anjānā min hādhihi la-nakūnanna minash-shākirīn.*

(63) Say, [O Prophet,] "Who rescues you from the darkest times on land and at sea? He [alone] you call upon with humility, openly and secretly: 'If You rescue us from this, we will be ever grateful.'"

◆━◆

قُلِ ٱللَّهُ يُنَجِّيكُم مِّنْهَا وَمِن كُلِّ كَرْبٍ ثُمَّ أَنتُمْ تُشْرِكُونَ ۝

(64) *Quli-llāhu yunajjīkum minhā wa-min kulli karbin thumma antum tushrikūn.*

(64) Say, "[Only] Allah rescues you from this and any other distress, yet you associate others with Him [in worship]."

◆━◆

قُل هُوَ ٱلْقَادِرُ عَلَىٰ أَن يَبْعَثَ عَلَيْكُمْ عَذَابًا مِّن فَوْقِكُمْ أَوْ مِن تَحْتِ أَرْجُلِكُمْ أَوْ يَلْبِسَكُمْ شِيَعًا وَيُذِيقَ بَعْضَكُم بَأْسَ بَعْضٍ ۗ ٱنظُرْ كَيْفَ نُصَرِّفُ ٱلْآيَٰتِ لَعَلَّهُمْ يَفْقَهُونَ ﴿٦٥﴾

⑥⑤ *Qul huwal-qādiru ‘alā an yab‘atha ‘alaykum ‘adhāban min fawqikum aw min taḥti arjulikum aw yalbisakum shiya‘an wa-yudhīqa ba‘ḍakum ba‘sa ba‘ḍ; unẓur kayfa nuṣarriful-āyāti la‘allahum yafqahūn.*

⑥⑤ Say, "He [alone] has the power to unleash upon you a torment from above or below you or split you into [conflicting] factions and make you taste the violence of one another." See how We vary the signs, so perhaps they will comprehend.

❖

وَكَذَّبَ بِهِۦ قَوْمُكَ وَهُوَ ٱلْحَقُّ ۚ قُل لَّسْتُ عَلَيْكُم بِوَكِيلٍ ﴿٦٦﴾

⑥⑥ *Wa-kadhdhaba bihi qawmuka wa-huwal-ḥaqq; qul lastu ‘alaykum bi-wakīl.*

⑥⑥ Still your people, [O Prophet,] have rejected this [Quran], although it is the truth. Say, "I am not a keeper over you."

❖

لِّكُلِّ نَبَإٍ مُّسْتَقَرٌّ ۚ وَسَوْفَ تَعْلَمُونَ ﴿٦٧﴾

⑥⑦ *Li-kulli naba'in mustaqarrun wa-sawfa ta‘lamūn.*

⑥⑦ Every [destined] matter has a [set] time to transpire. And you will soon come to know.

وَإِذَا رَأَيْتَ ٱلَّذِينَ يَخُوضُونَ فِى ءَايَـٰتِنَا فَأَعْرِضْ عَنْهُمْ حَتَّىٰ يَخُوضُواْ
فِى حَدِيثٍ غَيْرِهِۦ وَإِمَّا يُنسِيَنَّكَ ٱلشَّيْطَـٰنُ فَلَا تَقْعُدْ بَعْدَ ٱلذِّكْرَىٰ
مَعَ ٱلْقَوْمِ ٱلظَّـٰلِمِينَ ۝

68 *Wa-idhā ra'ayta-lladhīna yakhūḍūna fī āyātinā fa-a'riḍ 'anhum
ḥattā yakhūḍū fī ḥadīthin ghayrihi wa-immā yunsiyannakash-
shayṭānu fa-lā taq'ud ba'dadh-dhikrā ma'al-qawmiẓ-ẓālimīn.*

68 And when you come across those who ridicule Our revelations,
do not sit with them unless they engage in a different topic. Should
Satan make you forget, then once you remember, do not [continue
to] sit with the wrongdoing people.

وَمَا عَلَى ٱلَّذِينَ يَتَّقُونَ مِنْ حِسَابِهِم مِّن شَىْءٍ وَلَـٰكِن ذِكْرَىٰ لَعَلَّهُمْ
يَتَّقُونَ ۝

69 *Wa-mā 'ala-lladhīna yattaqūna min ḥisābihim min shay'in wa-lākin
dhikrā la'allahum yattaqūn.*

69 Those mindful [of Allah] will not be accountable for those
[who ridicule it] whatsoever—their duty is to advise, so perhaps
the ridiculers will abstain.

وَذَرِ ٱلَّذِينَ ٱتَّخَذُواْ دِينَهُمْ لَعِبًا وَلَهْوًا وَغَرَّتْهُمُ ٱلْحَيَوٰةُ ٱلدُّنْيَا وَذَكِّرْ بِهِ أَن تُبْسَلَ نَفْسٌ بِمَا كَسَبَتْ لَيْسَ لَهَا مِن دُونِ ٱللَّهِ وَلِيٌّ وَلَا شَفِيعٌ وَإِن تَعْدِلْ كُلَّ عَدْلٍ لَّا يُؤْخَذْ مِنْهَا أُوْلَٰئِكَ ٱلَّذِينَ أُبْسِلُواْ بِمَا كَسَبُواْ لَهُمْ شَرَابٌ مِّنْ حَمِيمٍ وَعَذَابٌ أَلِيمٌ بِمَا كَانُواْ يَكْفُرُونَ ۝

70 *Wa-dhari-lladhīna-ttakhadhū dīnahum laʿiban wa-lahwan wa-gharrat-humul-ḥayātud-dunyā wa-dhakkir bihi an tubsala nafsun bimā kasabat laysa lahā min dūni-llāhi walīyyun wa-lā shafīʿun wa-in taʿdil kulla ʿadlin lā yuʾkhadh minhā; ulāʾika-lladhīna ub-silū bimā kasabū; lahum sharābum min ḥamīmin wa-ʿadhābun alīmun bimā kānū yakfurūn.*

70 And leave those who take this faith [of Islam] as mere play and amusement and are deluded by [their] worldly life. Yet remind them by this [Quran], so no one should be ruined for their misdeeds. They will have no protector or intercessor other than Allah. Even if they were to offer every [possible] ransom, none will be accepted from them. Those are the ones who will be ruined for their misdeeds. They will have a boiling drink and painful punishment for their disbelief.

قُلْ أَنَدْعُواْ مِن دُونِ ٱللَّهِ مَا لَا يَنفَعُنَا وَلَا يَضُرُّنَا وَنُرَدُّ عَلَىٰٓ أَعْقَابِنَا بَعْدَ إِذْ هَدَىٰنَا ٱللَّهُ كَٱلَّذِى ٱسْتَهْوَتْهُ ٱلشَّيَـٰطِينُ فِى ٱلْأَرْضِ حَيْرَانَ لَهُۥٓ أَصْحَـٰبٌ يَدْعُونَهُۥٓ إِلَى ٱلْهُدَى ٱئْتِنَا قُلْ إِنَّ هُدَى ٱللَّهِ هُوَ ٱلْهُدَىٰ وَأُمِرْنَا لِنُسْلِمَ لِرَبِّ ٱلْعَـٰلَمِينَ ۝

Qul: a-nad‘ū min dūni-llāhi mā lā yanfa‘unā wa-lā yaḍurrunā wa-nuraddu ‘alā a‘qābinā ba‘da idh hadāna-llāhu ka-lladhi-istahwat-hush-shayāṭīnu fil-arḍi ḥayrāna lahu aṣḥābun yad‘ūnahū ilal-huda-’tinā; qul inna huda-llāhi huwal-hudā wa-umirnā li-nuslima li-rabbil-‘ālamīn.

Ask [them, O Prophet], "Should we invoke, other than Allah, those [idols] which cannot benefit or harm us, and turn back to disbelief after Allah has guided us? [If we do so, we will be] like those disoriented by devils in the wilderness, while their companions call them to guidance, [saying], 'Come to us!'" Say, [O Prophet,] "Allah's guidance is the [only] true guidance. And we are commanded to submit to the Lord of all worlds.

وَأَنْ أَقِيمُواْ ٱلصَّلَوٰةَ وَٱتَّقُوهُ وَهُوَ ٱلَّذِىٓ إِلَيْهِ تُحْشَرُونَ ۝

Wa-an aqīmuṣ-ṣalāta wa-ttaqūhu wa-huwa-lladhī ilayhi tuḥsharūn.

Establish prayer, and be mindful of Him. To Him you will all be gathered together.

وَهُوَ ٱلَّذِى خَلَقَ ٱلسَّمَـٰوَتِ وَٱلْأَرْضَ بِٱلْحَقِّ وَيَوْمَ يَقُولُ كُن فَيَكُونُ قَوْلُهُ ٱلْحَقُّ وَلَهُ ٱلْمُلْكُ يَوْمَ يُنفَخُ فِى ٱلصُّورِ عَـٰلِمُ ٱلْغَيْبِ وَٱلشَّهَـٰدَةِ وَهُوَ ٱلْحَكِيمُ ٱلْخَبِيرُ ۝

(73) Wa-huwa-lladhī khalaqas-samāwāti wal-arḍa bil-ḥaqqi wa-yawma yaqūlu kun fa-yakūn; qawluhul-ḥaqq wa-lahul-mulku yawma yunfakhu fil-ṣūr; ʿālimul-ghaybi wash-shahādati wa-huwal-ḥakīmul-khabīr.

(73) He is the One who created the heavens and the earth in truth. On the Day [of Judgment] He will say, 'Be!' And there will be! His command is truth. All authority is His [alone] on the Day the Trumpet will be blown. He is the Knower of all—seen or unseen. And He is the All-Wise, All-Aware."

Pause here and read

اللَّهُمَّ بِحَقِّ سِرِّ هَذِهِ الْأَسْرَارِ وَبِحَقِّ كَرَمِكَ الْخَفِيِّ وَبِحَقِّ اسْمِكَ الْعَظِيمِ أَنْ تَقْضِيَ حَاجَاتِنَا وَحَاجَاتِ الْحَاضِرِينَ يَا قَاضِيَ الْحَاجَاتِ يَا أَرْحَمَ الرَّاحِمِينَ قَوْلُكَ الْحَقّ.

Allāhumma bi-ḥaqqi sirri hādhihil-asrār, wa-bi-ḥaqqi karamikal-khafiyy, wa-bi-ḥaqqismikal-ʿaẓīm, an taqḍiya ḥājātinā wa-ḥājātil-ḥāḍirīn, yā qāḍiyal-ḥājāt, yā arḥamar-rāḥimīn, qawlukal-ḥaqq.

O Allah, I ask You by the status of the secrets of the unseen, and by the status of Your hidden generosity, and by the status of Your great name that You fulfill our needs and the needs of all those present, O You who fulfill all needs, O Most Merciful of all those who show mercy. Your words are true.

وَإِذْ قَالَ إِبْرَٰهِيمُ لِأَبِيهِ ءَازَرَ أَتَتَّخِذُ أَصْنَامًا ءَالِهَةً إِنِّي أَرَىٰكَ وَقَوْمَكَ فِي ضَلَٰلٍ مُّبِينٍ ۝

(74) *Wa-idh qāla Ibrāhīmu li-abīhi Āzara a-tattakhidhu aṣnāman ālihatan innī arāka wa-qawmaka fī ḍalālin mubīn.*

(74) And [remember] when Abraham said to his father, Azar, "Do you take idols as gods? It is clear to me that you and your people are entirely misguided."

وَكَذَٰلِكَ نُرِىٓ إِبْرَٰهِيمَ مَلَكُوتَ ٱلسَّمَٰوَٰتِ وَٱلْأَرْضِ وَلِيَكُونَ مِنَ ٱلْمُوقِنِينَ ۝

(75) *Wa-ka-dhālika nurī Ibrāhīma malakūtas-samāwāti wal-arḍi wa-li-yakūna minal-mūqinīn.*

(75) We also showed Abraham the wonders of the heavens and the earth, so he would be sure in faith.

فَلَمَّا جَنَّ عَلَيْهِ ٱلَّيْلُ رَءَا كَوْكَبًا قَالَ هَٰذَا رَبِّي فَلَمَّآ أَفَلَ قَالَ لَآ أُحِبُّ ٱلْءَافِلِينَ ۝

(76) *Fa-lammā janna ʿalayhil-laylu raʾā kawkaban qāla hādhā rabbī fa-lammā afala qāla lā uḥibbu al-āfilīn.*

(76) When the night grew dark upon him, he saw a star and said, "This is my Lord!" But when it set, he said, "I do not love things that set."

فَلَمَّا رَءَا ٱلْقَمَرَ بَازِغًا قَالَ هَٰذَا رَبِّى فَلَمَّآ أَفَلَ قَالَ لَئِن لَّمْ يَهْدِنِى رَبِّى لَأَكُونَنَّ مِنَ ٱلْقَوْمِ ٱلضَّآلِّينَ ۝

Fa-lammā ra'al-qamara bāzighan qāla hādhā rabbī fa-lammā afala qāla la-in lam yahdinī rabbī la-akūnanna minal-qawmiḍ-ḍāllīn.

⑦⑦ Then when he saw the moon rising, he said, "This one is my Lord!" But when it disappeared, he said, "If my Lord does not guide me, I will certainly be one of the misguided people."

◆━◆━◆

فَلَمَّا رَءَا ٱلشَّمْسَ بَازِغَةً قَالَ هَٰذَا رَبِّى هَٰذَآ أَكْبَرُ فَلَمَّآ أَفَلَتْ قَالَ يَٰقَوْمِ إِنِّى بَرِىٓءٌ مِّمَّا تُشْرِكُونَ ۝

Fa-lammā ra'ash-shamsa bāzighatan qāla hādhā rabbī hādhā akbaru fa-lammā afalat qāla yā qawmi innī barī'un mimmā tushrikūn.

⑦⑧ Then when he saw the sun shining, he said, "This must be my Lord—it is the greatest!" But again when it set, he declared, "O my people! I totally reject whatever you associate [with Allah in worship].

◆━◆━◆

إِنِّى وَجَّهْتُ وَجْهِىَ لِلَّذِى فَطَرَ ٱلسَّمَٰوَٰتِ وَٱلْأَرْضَ حَنِيفًا وَمَآ أَنَا۠ مِنَ ٱلْمُشْرِكِينَ ۝

Innī wajahtu wajhiya li-lladhī faṭaras-samāwāti wal-arḍa ḥanīfan wa-mā ana minal-mushrikīn.

⑦⑨ I have turned my face toward the One who has originated the heavens and the earth—being upright—and I am not one of the polytheists."

وَحَآجَّهُۥ قَوْمُهُۥ قَالَ أَتُحَـٰٓجُّوٓنِّى فِى ٱللَّهِ وَقَدْ هَدَٰنِ وَلَآ أَخَافُ مَا تُشْرِكُونَ بِهِۦٓ إِلَّآ أَن يَشَآءَ رَبِّى شَيْـًٔا وَسِعَ رَبِّى كُلَّ شَىْءٍ عِلْمًا أَفَلَا تَتَذَكَّرُونَ ۝

Wa-ḥāj-jahu qawmuhu qāla a-tuḥājjūnnī fi-llāhi wa-qad hadāni wa-lā akhāfu mā tushrikūna bihī illā an yashā'a rabbī shay'an wasi'a rabbī kulla shay'in 'ilman a-fa-lā tatadhakkarūn?

And his people argued with him. He responded, "Are you arguing with me about Allah, while He has guided me? I am not afraid of whatever [idols] you associate with Him—[none can harm me], unless my Lord so wills. My Lord encompasses everything in [His] knowledge. Will you not be mindful?

◆—◆

وَكَيْفَ أَخَافُ مَآ أَشْرَكْتُمْ وَلَا تَخَافُونَ أَنَّكُمْ أَشْرَكْتُم بِٱللَّهِ مَا لَمْ يُنَزِّلْ بِهِۦ عَلَيْكُمْ سُلْطَٰنًا فَأَىُّ ٱلْفَرِيقَيْنِ أَحَقُّ بِٱلْأَمْنِ إِن كُنتُمْ تَعْلَمُونَ ۝

Wa-kayfa akhāfu mā ashraktum wa-lā takhāfūna annakum ashraktum bi-llāhi mā lam yunazzil bihi 'alaykum sulṭānan fa-ayyul-farīqayni aḥaqqu bil-amni in kuntum ta'lamūn.

And how should I fear your associate-gods, while you have no fear in associating [others] with Allah—a practice He has never authorized? Which side has more right to security? [Tell me] if you really know!"

◆—◆

اَلَّذِينَ ءَامَنُواْ وَلَمْ يَلْبِسُوٓاْ إِيمَٰنَهُم بِظُلْمٍ أُوْلَٰٓئِكَ لَهُمُ ٱلْأَمْنُ وَهُم مُّهْتَدُونَ ۝

٨٢ *Alladhīna āmanū wa-lam yalbisū īmānahum bi-ẓulmin ulāʾika lahumul-amnu wa-hum muhtadūn.*

٨٢ It is [only] those who are faithful and do not tarnish their faith with falsehood who are guaranteed security and are [rightly] guided.

وَتِلْكَ حُجَّتُنَآ ءَاتَيْنَٰهَآ إِبْرَٰهِيمَ عَلَىٰ قَوْمِهِۦ نَرْفَعُ دَرَجَٰتٍ مَّن نَّشَآءُ إِنَّ رَبَّكَ حَكِيمٌ عَلِيمٌ ۝

٨٣ *Wa-tilka ḥujjatunā ātaynāhā Ibrāhīma ʿalā qawmih narfaʿu darajātin man nashāʾ inna rabbaka ḥakīmun ʿalīm.*

٨٣ This was the argument We gave Abraham against his people. We elevate in rank whoever We please. Surely your Lord is All-Wise, All-Knowing.

وَوَهَبْنَا لَهُۥٓ إِسْحَٰقَ وَيَعْقُوبَ كُلًّا هَدَيْنَا وَنُوحًا هَدَيْنَا مِن قَبْلُ وَمِن ذُرِّيَّتِهِۦ دَاوُۥدَ وَسُلَيْمَٰنَ وَأَيُّوبَ وَيُوسُفَ وَمُوسَىٰ وَهَٰرُونَ وَكَذَٰلِكَ نَجْزِى ٱلْمُحْسِنِينَ ۝

٨٤ *Wa-wahabnā lahū Isḥāqa wa-Yaʿqūba kullan hadaynā wa-Nūḥan hadaynā min qablu wa-min dhurriyyatihi Dāwūda wa-Sulaymāna wa-Ayyūba wa-Yūsufa wa-Mūsā wa-Hārūna wa-ka-dhālika najzil-muḥsinīn.*

٨٤ And We blessed him with Isaac and Jacob. We guided them all as We previously guided Noah and those among his descendants: David, Solomon, Job, Joseph, Moses, and Aaron. This is how We reward the good-doers.

وَزَكَرِيَّا وَيَحْيَىٰ وَعِيسَىٰ وَإِلْيَاسَ كُلٌّ مِّنَ ٱلصَّٰلِحِينَ ۝

(85) *Wa-Zakariyyā wa-Yaḥyā wa-ʿĪsā wa-Ilyāsa kullun minaṣ-ṣāliḥīn.*

(85) Likewise, [We guided] Zachariah, John, Jesus, and Elias, who were all of the righteous.

◆━◆

وَإِسْمَٰعِيلَ وَٱلْيَسَعَ وَيُونُسَ وَلُوطًا وَكُلًّا فَضَّلْنَا عَلَى ٱلْعَٰلَمِينَ ۝

(86) *Wa-Ismāʿīla wal-Yasaʿa wa-Yūnusa wa-Lūṭan wa-kullan faḍḍalnā ʿalal-ʿālamīn.*

(86) [We also guided] Ishmael, Elisha, Jonah, and Lot, favoring each over other people [of their time].

◆━◆

وَمِنْ ءَابَآئِهِمْ وَذُرِّيَّٰتِهِمْ وَإِخْوَٰنِهِمْ وَٱجْتَبَيْنَٰهُمْ وَهَدَيْنَٰهُمْ إِلَىٰ صِرَٰطٍ مُّسْتَقِيمٍ ۝

(87) *Wa-min ābāʾihim wa-dhurriyyātihim wa-ikhwānihim wa-jtabaynāhum wa-hadaynāhum ilā ṣirāṭim-mustaqīm.*

(87) And [We favored] some of their forefathers, their descendants, and their brothers. We chose them and guided them to the Straight Path.

Pause here and read 41 times

﴿ وَأُفَوِّضُ أَمْرِي إِلَى ٱللَّهِ إِنَّ ٱللَّهَ بَصِيرٌ بِٱلْعِبَادِ ﴾

﴿ *Wa-ufawwiḍu amrī ila-Allāh; inna-Allāha baṣīrun bil-ʿibād.* ﴾

﴿ And I entrust my affairs to Allah; indeed
Allah is ever observant of His servants. ﴾

Then with pleading earnestness read

﴿ رَبَّنَا آتِنَا فِي الدُّنْيَا حَسَنَةً وَفِي الآخِرَةِ حَسَنَةً وَقِنَا عَذَابَ النَّارِ ﴾

❋ *Rabbānā ātinā fid-dunyā ḥasanatan wa-fil-ākhirati ḥasanatan wa-qinā 'adhāban-nār.* ❋

❋ Our Lord, grant us in this world favor and in the hereafter favor, and protect us from the punishment of the fire. ❋

Then read

اللَّهُمَّ إِنِّي أَسْأَلُكَ بِحَقِّ هَؤُلَاءِ الأَنْبِيَاءِ وَالمُرْسَلِينَ وَبِحُرْمَةِ سَيِّدِ الأَنْبِيَاءِ سَيِّدِنَا مُحَمَّدٍ رَسُولِكَ خَاتَمِ النَّبِيِّينَ وَآلِهِ وَصَحْبِهِ الطَّيِّبِينَ الطَّاهِرِينَ أَنْ تَقْضِيَ حَاجَاتِنَا وَحَاجَاتِ الحَاضِرِينَ يَا قَاضِيَ الحَاجَاتِ يَا أَرْحَمَ الرَّاحِمِين.

Allāhumma innī as'aluka bi-ḥaqqi hā'ulā'il-anbiyā'i wal-mursalīn, wa-bi-ḥurmati sayyidil-anbiyā'i sayyidinā Muḥammadin rasūlika khātamin-nabiyyīn, wa-ālihi wa-ṣaḥbihiṭ-ṭayyibīnaṭ-ṭāhirīn, an taqḍiya ḥājātinā wa-ḥājātil-ḥāḍirīn, yā qāḍiyal-ḥājāt, yā arḥamar-rāḥimīn.

O Allah, I ask you by the status of all of these prophets and messengers and by the sanctity of the master of all prophets, Prophet Muhammad, Your messenger and the seal of the prophets, and his family and his righteous and pure companions that You fulfill our needs and the needs of all those present. O You who fulfill all needs, O Most Merciful of those who show mercy.

ذَٰلِكَ هُدَى ٱللَّهِ يَهْدِى بِهِۦ مَن يَشَآءُ مِنْ عِبَادِهِۦ وَلَوْ أَشْرَكُوا۟ لَحَبِطَ عَنْهُم مَّا كَانُوا۟ يَعْمَلُونَ ۝

(88) *Dhālika huda-llāhi yahdī bihi man yashā'u min 'ibādihi wa-law ashrakū la-ḥabiṭa 'anhum mā kānū ya'malūn.*

(88) This is Allah's guidance with which He guides whoever He wills of His servants. Had they associated others with Him [in worship], their [good] deeds would have been wasted.

◆—◆

أُو۟لَٰٓئِكَ ٱلَّذِينَ ءَاتَيْنَٰهُمُ ٱلْكِتَٰبَ وَٱلْحُكْمَ وَٱلنُّبُوَّةَ فَإِن يَكْفُرْ بِهَا هَٰٓؤُلَآءِ فَقَدْ وَكَّلْنَا بِهَا قَوْمًا لَّيْسُوا۟ بِهَا بِكَٰفِرِينَ ۝

(89) *Ulā'ika-lladhīna ātaynā-humul-kitāba wal-ḥukma wan-nubuwwata fa-in yakfur bihā hā'ulā'i faqad wakkalnā bihā qawman laysū bihā bi-kāfirīn.*

(89) Those were the ones to whom We gave the Scripture, wisdom, and prophethood. But if these [pagans] disbelieve in this [message], then We have already entrusted it to a people who will never disbelieve in it.

◆—◆

أُو۟لَٰٓئِكَ ٱلَّذِينَ هَدَى ٱللَّهُ فَبِهُدَىٰهُمُ ٱقْتَدِهْ قُل لَّآ أَسْـَٔلُكُمْ عَلَيْهِ أَجْرًا إِنْ هُوَ إِلَّا ذِكْرَىٰ لِلْعَٰلَمِينَ ۝

(90) *Ulā'ika-lladhīna hada-Allāhu fa-bihudāhum iqtadih qul-lā as'alukum 'alayhi ajran in huwa illā dhikrā lil-'ālamīn.*

(90) These [prophets] were [rightly] guided by Allah, so follow their guidance. Say, "I ask no reward of you for this [Quran]—it is a reminder to the whole world."

Pause here and read 41 times

اللَّهُمَّ إِيَّاكَ نَعْبُدُ وَإِيَّاكَ نَسْتَعِينُ اللَّهُمَّ صَلِّ عَلَى سَيِّدِنَا مُحَمَّدٍ وَآلِ سَيِّدِنَا مُحَمَّدٍ وَصَلِّ عَلَى جَمِيعِ الْأَنْبِيَاءِ وَالْمُرْسَلِينَ يَا رَحْمٰنَ الدُّنْيَا وَالاخِرَةِ وَرَحِيمَهُمَا تُعْطِيهِمَا مَنْ تَشَاءُ وَتَمْنَعُهُمَا عَمَّنْ تَشَاءُ اللَّهُمَّ اِرْحَمْنَا رَحْمَةً تُغْنِنَا بِهَا عَنْ رَحْمَةِ مَنْ سِوَاكَ يَا أَرْحَمَ الرَّاحِمِينَ.

Allāhumma iyyāka naʿbudu wa-iyyāka nastaʿīn. Allāhumma ṣalli ʿalā sayyidinā Muḥammadin wa-āli sayyidinā Muḥammad, wa-ṣalli ʿalā jamīʿil-anbiyāʾi wal-mursalīn. Yā Raḥmānad-dunyā wal-ākhira wa-raḥīmahumā, tuʿṭīhimā man tashāʾu wa-tamnaʿuhumā ʿamman tashāʾ. Allāhumma irḥamnā raḥmatan tughninā bihā ʿan raḥmati man siwāk. Yā arḥamar-rāḥimīn.

O Allah, You alone do we worship and You alone do we ask for help. O Allah, send Your prayers on Prophet Muhammad and on the family of Prophet Muhammad, and send your prayers on all of the prophets and messengers. O You who are the Compassionate and the Merciful in both this world and the hereafter. You give mercy to whomever You wish and withhold it from whomever You wish. O Allah, be merciful with us in a way that suffices us, such that we don't need the mercy of others. O Most Merciful of all those who show mercy.

وَمَا قَدَرُواْ ٱللَّهَ حَقَّ قَدْرِهِۦ إِذْ قَالُواْ مَآ أَنزَلَ ٱللَّهُ عَلَىٰ بَشَرٍ مِّن شَىْءٍ قُلْ مَنْ أَنزَلَ ٱلْكِتَـٰبَ ٱلَّذِى جَآءَ بِهِۦ مُوسَىٰ نُورًا وَهُدًى لِّلنَّاسِ تَجْعَلُونَهُۥ قَرَاطِيسَ تُبْدُونَهَا وَتُخْفُونَ كَثِيرًا وَعُلِّمْتُم مَّا لَمْ تَعْلَمُوٓاْ أَنتُمْ وَلَآ ءَابَآؤُكُمْ قُلِ ٱللَّهُ ثُمَّ ذَرْهُمْ فِى خَوْضِهِمْ يَلْعَبُونَ ﴿٩١﴾

(91) *Wa-mā qadaru-llāha ḥaqqa qadrihi idh qālū mā anzala-Allāhu ‘alā basharin min shay’in qul man anzalal-kitāba-lladhī jā’a bihi Mūsā nūran wa-hudal-lin-nāsi taj‘alūnahu qarāṭīsa tubdūnahā wa-tukhfūna kathīran wa-‘ullimtum mā lam ta‘lamū antum wa-lā ābā’ukum quli-llāhu thumma dharhum fī khawḍihim yal‘abūn.*

(91) And they have not shown Allah His proper reverence when they said, "Allah has revealed nothing to any human being." Say, [O Prophet,] "Who then revealed the Book brought forth by Moses as a light and guidance for people, which you split into separate sheets—revealing some and hiding much? You have been taught [through this Quran] what neither you nor your forefathers knew." Say, [O Prophet,] "Allah [revealed it]!" Then leave them to amuse themselves with falsehood.

◆━◆

وَهَـٰذَا كِتَـٰبٌ أَنزَلْنَـٰهُ مُبَارَكٌ مُّصَدِّقُ ٱلَّذِى بَيْنَ يَدَيْهِ وَلِتُنذِرَ أُمَّ ٱلْقُرَىٰ وَمَنْ حَوْلَهَا وَٱلَّذِينَ يُؤْمِنُونَ بِٱلْءَاخِرَةِ يُؤْمِنُونَ بِهِۦ وَهُمْ عَلَىٰ صَلَاتِهِمْ يُحَافِظُونَ ﴿٩٢﴾

(92) *Wa-hādhā kitābun anzalnāhu mubārakun muṣaddiqu-lladhī bayna yadayhi wa-li-tundhira ummal-qurā wa-man ḥawlahā wa-alladhīna yu’minūna bil-ākhirati yu’minūna bihi wa-hum ‘alā ṣalātihim yūḥāfiẓūn.*

(92) This is a blessed Book which We have revealed—confirming what came before it—so you may warn the Mother of Cities and everyone around it. Those who believe in the Hereafter [truly] believe in it and guard their prayers.

وَمَنْ أَظْلَمُ مِمَّنِ ٱفْتَرَىٰ عَلَى ٱللَّهِ كَذِبًا أَوْ قَالَ أُوحِىَ إِلَيَّ وَلَمْ يُوحَ إِلَيْهِ شَىْءٌ وَمَن قَالَ سَأُنزِلُ مِثْلَ مَآ أَنزَلَ ٱللَّهُ وَلَوْ تَرَىٰ إِذِ ٱلظَّالِمُونَ فِى غَمَرَٰتِ ٱلْمَوْتِ وَٱلْمَلَـٰٓئِكَةُ بَاسِطُوٓا۟ أَيْدِيهِمْ أَخْرِجُوٓا۟ أَنفُسَكُمُ ٱلْيَوْمَ تُجْزَوْنَ عَذَابَ ٱلْهُونِ بِمَا كُنتُمْ تَقُولُونَ عَلَى ٱللَّهِ غَيْرَ ٱلْحَقِّ وَكُنتُمْ عَنْ ءَايَـٰتِهِۦ تَسْتَكْبِرُونَ ۝٩٣

(93) Wa-man aẓlamu mimman iftarā ‘ala-Allāhi kadhiban aw qāla ūḥiya ilayya wa-lam yūḥa ilayhi shay’un wa-man qāla sa-unzilu mithla mā anzala-Allāhu wa-law tarā idhiẓ-ẓālimūna fī gharamātil-mawti wal-malā’ikatu bāsiṭū aydīhim akhrijū anfusakumul-yawma tujzawna ‘adhābal-hūni bimā kuntum taqūlūna ‘ala-llāhi ghayral-ḥaqqi wa-kuntum ‘an āyātihi tastakbirūn.

(93) Who does more wrong than the one who fabricates lies against Allah or claims, "I have received revelations!"—although nothing was revealed to them—or the one who says, "I can reveal the like of Allah's revelations!"? If you, [O Prophet,] could only see the wrongdoers in the throes of death while the angels are stretching out their hands [saying], "Give up your souls! Today you will be rewarded with the torment of disgrace for telling lies about Allah and for being arrogant toward His revelations!"

وَلَقَدْ جِئْتُمُونَا فُرَادَىٰ كَمَا خَلَقْنَـٰكُمْ أَوَّلَ مَرَّةٍ وَتَرَكْتُم مَّا خَوَّلْنَـٰكُمْ وَرَآءَ ظُهُورِكُمْ وَمَا نَرَىٰ مَعَكُمْ شُفَعَآءَكُمُ ٱلَّذِينَ زَعَمْتُمْ أَنَّهُمْ فِيكُمْ شُرَكَـٰٓؤُا۟ لَقَد تَّقَطَّعَ بَيْنَكُمْ وَضَلَّ عَنكُم مَّا كُنتُمْ تَزْعُمُونَ ﴿٩٤﴾

(94) *Wa-la-qad ji'tumūnā furādā ka-mā khalaqnākum awwala marratin wa-taraktum mā khawwalnākum warā'a ẓuhūrikum wa-mā narā maʿakum shufaʿā'akumu-lladhīna zaʿamtum annahum fīkum shurakā' la-qad taqaṭṭaʿa baynakum wa-ḍalla ʿankum mā kuntum tazʿumūn.*

(94) [Today] you have come back to Us all alone as We created you the first time—leaving behind everything We have provided you with. We do not see your intercessors with you—those you claimed were Allah's partners [in worship]. All your ties have been broken and all your claims have let you down.

＊ إِنَّ ٱللَّهَ فَالِقُ ٱلْحَبِّ وَٱلنَّوَىٰ يُخْرِجُ ٱلْحَىَّ مِنَ ٱلْمَيِّتِ وَمُخْرِجُ ٱلْمَيِّتِ مِنَ ٱلْحَىِّ ذَٰلِكُمُ ٱللَّهُ فَأَنَّىٰ تُؤْفَكُونَ ﴿٩٥﴾

(95) *Inna-Allāha fāliqul-ḥabbi wan-nawā yukhrijul-ḥayya minal-mayyiti wa-mukhrijul-mayyiti minal-ḥayyi dhālikumu-llāhu fa-annā tu'fakūn.*

(95) Indeed, Allah is the One who causes seeds and fruit stones to sprout. He brings forth the living from the dead and the dead from the living. That is Allah! How can you then be deluded [from the truth]?

فَالِقُ ٱلْإِصْبَاحِ وَجَعَلَ ٱلَّيْلَ سَكَنًا وَٱلشَّمْسَ وَٱلْقَمَرَ حُسْبَانًا ۚ ذَٰلِكَ تَقْدِيرُ ٱلْعَزِيزِ ٱلْعَلِيمِ ﴿٩٦﴾

(96) *Fāliqul-iṣbāḥi wa-jaʿalal-layla sakanan wash-shamsa wal-qamara ḥusbānan dhālika taqdīrul-ʿazīzil-ʿalīm.*

(96) He causes the dawn to break and has [made] the night for rest and made the sun and the moon [to travel] with precision. That is the design of the Almighty, All-Knowing.

وَهُوَ ٱلَّذِى جَعَلَ لَكُمُ ٱلنُّجُومَ لِتَهْتَدُواْ بِهَا فِى ظُلُمَٰتِ ٱلْبَرِّ وَٱلْبَحْرِ ۗ قَدْ فَصَّلْنَا ٱلْءَايَٰتِ لِقَوْمٍ يَعْلَمُونَ ﴿٩٧﴾

(97) *Wa-huwa-lladhī jaʿala lakumun-nujūma li-tahtadū bihā fī ẓulumātil-barri wal-baḥri qad faṣṣalnal-āyāti li-qawmin yaʿlamūn.*

(97) And He is the One who has made the stars as your guide through the darkness of land and sea. We have already made the signs clear for people who know.

وَهُوَ ٱلَّذِى أَنشَأَكُم مِّن نَّفْسٍ وَٰحِدَةٍ فَمُسْتَقَرٌّ وَمُسْتَوْدَعٌ ۗ قَدْ فَصَّلْنَا ٱلْءَايَٰتِ لِقَوْمٍ يَفْقَهُونَ ﴿٩٨﴾

(98) *Wa-huwa-lladhī ansha’akum min nafsin wāḥidatin fa-mustaqarrun wa-mustawdaʿun qad faṣṣalnal-āyāti li-qawmin yafqahūn.*

(98) And He is the One who originated you all from a single soul, then assigned you a place to live and another to [be laid to] rest. We have already made the signs clear for people who comprehend.

وَهُوَ ٱلَّذِىٓ أَنزَلَ مِنَ ٱلسَّمَآءِ مَآءً فَأَخْرَجْنَا بِهِۦ نَبَاتَ كُلِّ شَىْءٍ فَأَخْرَجْنَا مِنْهُ خَضِرًا نُّخْرِجُ مِنْهُ حَبًّا مُّتَرَاكِبًا وَمِنَ ٱلنَّخْلِ مِن طَلْعِهَا قِنْوَانٌ دَانِيَةٌ وَجَنَّٰتٍ مِّنْ أَعْنَابٍ وَٱلزَّيْتُونَ وَٱلرُّمَّانَ مُشْتَبِهًا وَغَيْرَ مُتَشَٰبِهٍ ٱنظُرُوٓا۟ إِلَىٰ ثَمَرِهِۦٓ إِذَآ أَثْمَرَ وَيَنْعِهِۦٓ إِنَّ فِى ذَٰلِكُمْ لَءَايَٰتٍ لِّقَوْمٍ يُؤْمِنُونَ ۝

(99) *Wa-huwa-lladhī anzala minas-samā'i mā'an fa-akhrajnā bihi nabāta kulli shay'in fa-akhrajnā minhu khaḍiran nukhriju minhu ḥabban mutarākiban wa-minan-nakhli min ṭal'ihā qinwānun dāniyatun wa-jannātin min a'nābin waz-zaytūna war-rummāna mush-tabihan wa-ghayra mutashābihin unẓurū ilā thamarihi idhā athmara wa-yan'ihi inna fī dhālikum la-āyātil-li-qawmin yu'minūn.*

(99) And He is the One who sends down rain from the sky—causing all kinds of plants to grow—producing green stalks from which We bring forth clustered grain. And from palm trees come clusters of dates hanging within reach. [There are] also gardens of grapevines, olives, and pomegranates, similar [in shape] but dissimilar [in taste]. Look at their fruit as it yields and ripens! Indeed, in these are signs for people who believe.

◄━━►

وَجَعَلُوا۟ لِلَّهِ شُرَكَآءَ ٱلْجِنَّ وَخَلَقَهُمْ وَخَرَقُوا۟ لَهُۥ بَنِينَ وَبَنَٰتٍ بِغَيْرِ عِلْمٍ سُبْحَٰنَهُۥ وَتَعَٰلَىٰ عَمَّا يَصِفُونَ ۝

(100) *Wa-ja'alū li-llāhi shurakā'al-jinna wa-khalaqahum wa-kharaqū lahu banīna wa-banātin bi-ghayri 'ilmin subḥānahu wa-ta'ālā 'ammā yaṣifūn.*

(100) Yet they associate the jinn with Allah [in worship], even though He created them, and they falsely attribute to Him sons and daughters out of ignorance. Glorified and Exalted is He above what they claim!

بَدِيعُ ٱلسَّمَـٰوَٰتِ وَٱلْأَرْضِ ۖ أَنَّىٰ يَكُونُ لَهُۥ وَلَدٌ وَلَمْ تَكُن لَّهُۥ صَـٰحِبَةٌ ۖ وَخَلَقَ كُلَّ شَىْءٍ ۖ وَهُوَ بِكُلِّ شَىْءٍ عَلِيمٌ ۞

(101) *Badī‘us-samāwāti wal-arḍi annā yakūnu lahu waladun wa-lam takun lahu ṣāḥibatun wa-khalaqa kulla shay’in wa-huwa bi-kulli shay’in ‘alīm.*

(101) [He is] the Originator of the heavens and earth. How could He have children when He has no mate? He created all things and has [perfect] knowledge of everything.

❮◆❯

ذَٰلِكُمُ ٱللَّهُ رَبُّكُمْ ۖ لَآ إِلَـٰهَ إِلَّا هُوَ ۖ خَـٰلِقُ كُلِّ شَىْءٍ فَٱعْبُدُوهُ ۚ وَهُوَ عَلَىٰ كُلِّ شَىْءٍ وَكِيلٌ ۞

(102) *Dhālikumu-llāhu rabbukum lā ilāha illā huwa khāliqu kulli shay’in fa-‘budūhu wa-huwa ‘alā kulli shay’in wakīl.*

(102) That is Allah—your Lord! There is no god [worthy of worship] except Him. [He is] the Creator of all things, so worship Him [alone]. And He is the Maintainer of everything.

❮◆❯

لَّا تُدْرِكُهُ ٱلْأَبْصَـٰرُ وَهُوَ يُدْرِكُ ٱلْأَبْصَـٰرَ ۖ وَهُوَ ٱللَّطِيفُ ٱلْخَبِيرُ ۞

(103) *Lā tudrikuhul-abṣāru wa-huwa yudrikul-abṣāra wa-huwal-laṭīful-khabīr.*

(103) No vision can encompass Him, but He encompasses all vision. For He is the Most Subtle, All-Aware.

قَدْ جَاءَكُم بَصَائِرُ مِن رَّبِّكُمْ ۖ فَمَنْ أَبْصَرَ فَلِنَفْسِهِ ۖ وَمَنْ عَمِىَ فَعَلَيْهَا ۚ وَمَآ أَنَا۠ عَلَيْكُم بِحَفِيظٍ ﴿١٠٤﴾

⟨104⟩ *Qad jā'akum baṣā'iru min rabbikum fa-man abṣara fa-li-nafsihi wa-man 'amiya fa-'alayhā wa-mā anā 'alaykum bi-ḥafīẓ.*

⟨104⟩ Indeed, there have come to you insights from your Lord. So whoever chooses to see, it is for their own good. But whoever chooses to be blind, it is to their own loss. And I am not a keeper over you.

◆—◆

وَكَذَٰلِكَ نُصَرِّفُ ٱلْآيَٰتِ وَلِيَقُولُوا۟ دَرَسْتَ وَلِنُبَيِّنَهُۥ لِقَوْمٍ يَعْلَمُونَ ﴿١٠٥﴾

⟨105⟩ *Wa-ka-dhālika nuṣarriful-āyāti wa-li-yaqūlū darasta wa-li-nubayyinahu li-qawmin ya'lamūn.*

⟨105⟩ And so We vary our signs to the extent that they will say, "You have studied [previous scriptures]," and We make this [Quran] clear for people who know.

◆—◆

ٱتَّبِعْ مَآ أُوحِىَ إِلَيْكَ مِن رَّبِّكَ ۖ لَآ إِلَٰهَ إِلَّا هُوَ ۖ وَأَعْرِضْ عَنِ ٱلْمُشْرِكِينَ ﴿١٠٦﴾

⟨106⟩ *Ittabi' mā ūḥiya ilayka mir-rabbika lā ilāha illā huwa wa-a'riḍ 'anil-mushrikīn.*

⟨106⟩ [O Prophet!] Follow what is revealed to you from your Lord—there is no god [worthy of worship] except Him—and turn away from the polytheists.

وَلَوْ شَاءَ ٱللَّهُ مَآ أَشْرَكُوا۟ وَمَا جَعَلْنَٰكَ عَلَيْهِمْ حَفِيظًا وَمَآ أَنتَ عَلَيْهِم بِوَكِيلٍ ۝١٠٧

(107) *Wa-law shā'a-Allāhu mā ashrakū wa-mā ja'alnāka 'alayhim ḥafīẓan wa-mā anta 'alayhim bi-wakīl.*

(107) Had Allah willed, they would not have been polytheists. We have not appointed you as their keeper, nor are you their maintainer.

وَلَا تَسُبُّوا۟ ٱلَّذِينَ يَدْعُونَ مِن دُونِ ٱللَّهِ فَيَسُبُّوا۟ ٱللَّهَ عَدْوًۢا بِغَيْرِ عِلْمٍ كَذَٰلِكَ زَيَّنَّا لِكُلِّ أُمَّةٍ عَمَلَهُمْ ثُمَّ إِلَىٰ رَبِّهِم مَّرْجِعُهُمْ فَيُنَبِّئُهُم بِمَا كَانُوا۟ يَعْمَلُونَ ۝١٠٨

(108) *Wa-lā tasubbu-lladhīna yad'ūna min dūni-llāhi fa-yasubbu-llāha 'adwan bi-ghayri 'ilmin ka-dhālika zayyannā li-kulli ummatin 'amalahum thumma ilā rabbihim marji'uhum fa-yunabbi'uhum bimā kānū ya'malūn.*

(108) [O believers!] Do not insult what they invoke besides Allah, or they will insult Allah spitefully out of ignorance. This is how We have made each people's deeds appealing to them. Then to their Lord is their return, and He will inform them of what they used to do.

وَأَقْسَمُواْ بِٱللَّهِ جَهْدَ أَيْمَـٰنِهِمْ لَئِن جَآءَتْهُمْ ءَايَةٌ لَّيُؤْمِنُنَّ بِهَا قُلْ إِنَّمَا ٱلْأَيَـٰتُ عِندَ ٱللَّهِ وَمَا يُشْعِرُكُمْ أَنَّهَآ إِذَا جَآءَتْ لَا يُؤْمِنُونَ ۝

(109) *Wa-aqsamū bi-llāhi jahda aymānihim la-in jā'athum āyatul-la-yu'minunna bihā qul innamal-āyātu 'inda-Allāhi wa-mā yush'irukum annahā idhā jā'at lā yu'minūn.*

(109) They swear by Allah their most solemn oaths that if a sign were to come to them, they would certainly believe in it. Say, [O Prophet,] "Signs are only with Allah." What will make you [believers] realize that even if a sign were to come to them, they still would not believe?

وَنُقَلِّبُ أَفْـِٔدَتَهُمْ وَأَبْصَـٰرَهُمْ كَمَا لَمْ يُؤْمِنُواْ بِهِۦٓ أَوَّلَ مَرَّةٍ وَنَذَرُهُمْ فِى طُغْيَـٰنِهِمْ يَعْمَهُونَ ۝

(110) *Wa-nuqallibu af'idatahum wa-abṣārahum ka-mā lam yu'minū bihi awwala marratin wa-nadharuhum fī ṭughyānihim ya'mahūn.*

(110) We turn their hearts and eyes away [from the truth] as they refused to believe at first, leaving them to wander blindly in their defiance.

Pause here and read

اللَّهُمَّ يَا ذَا الْعَرْشِ الْكَرِيمِ وَالْمَلِكِ الْقَدِيمِ وَالْعَطَاءِ الْعَمِيمِ وَالْفَضْلِ الْعَظِيمِ وَالصِّرَاطِ الْمُسْتَقِيمِ يَا مُرْسِلَ اَلرِّيَاحِ يَا فَالِقَ الْإِصْبَاحِ يَا بَاعِثَ الْأَرْوَاحِ يَا ذَا الْجُودِ وَالسَّمَاحِ يَا اللّٰهَ يَا اللّٰهَ يَا اللّٰهَ يَا رَحْمَنُ يَا رَحْمَنُ يَا رَحْمَنُ يَا رَحِيمُ يَا رَحِيمُ يَا رَحِيمُ يَا أَحَدُ يَا صَمَدُ يَا فَرْدُ يَا وِتْرُ يَا حَيُّ يَا قَيُّومُ يَا ذَا الْجَلَالِ وَالْإِكْرَامِ ارْحَمْ ذُلَّنَا وَفَقْرَنَا وَفَاقَتَنَا وَانْفِرَادَنَا وَخُضُوعَنَا وَخُشُوعَنَا بَيْنَ يَدَيْكَ وَاعْتِمَادَنَا عَلَيْكَ وَتَضَرُّعَنَا إِلَيْكَ رَبِّ سَهِّلْ عَلَيْنَا كُلَّ عَسِيرٍ وَامْنَعْ عَنَّا شَرَّ كُلِّ ظَالِمٍ وَحَاسِدٍ وَآفَةٍ وَعَاهَةٍ وَمَرَضٍ وَبَلَاءٍ وَوَبَاءٍ وَطَاعُونٍ وَزَلْزَلَةٍ وَكلِّ شِدَّةٍ وَبَلِيَّةٍ يَا سُبُّوحُ يَا قُدُّوسُ يَا رَبَّ الْمَلَائِكَةِ وَالرُّوحِ وَصَلَّى اللّٰهَ عَلَى سَيِّدِنَا مُحَمَّدٍ وَعَلَى آلِهِ وَصَحْبِهِ وَسَلَّم.

Allāhumma yā dhal-‘arshil-karīm, wal-malikil-qadīm, wal-‘aṭā’il-‘amīm, wal-faḍlil-‘aẓīm, waṣ-ṣirāṭil-mustaqīm, yā mursilar-riyāḥ, yā fāliqal-iṣbāḥ, yā bā‘ithal-arwāḥ, yā dhal-jūdi was-samāḥ, yā Allāh, yā Allāh, yā Allāh, yā Raḥmān, yā Raḥmān, yā Raḥmān, yā Raḥīm, yā Raḥīm, yā Raḥīm, yā Aḥad, yā Ṣamad, yā Fard, yā Witr, yā Ḥayy, yā Qayyūm, yā dhal-jalāli wal-ikrām, irḥam dhullanā wa-faqranā wa-fāqatanā wa-infirādanā wa-khuḍū‘anā wa-khushū‘anā bayna yadayk, wa-i‘timādanā ‘alayk, wa-taḍarru‘anā ilayk. Rabbī sahhil ‘alaynā kulla ‘asīr, wa-mna‘ ‘annā sharra kulli ẓālimin wa-ḥāsidin wa-āfatin wa-‘āhatin wa-maraḍin wa-balā’in wa-wabā’in wa-ṭā‘ūnin wa-zalzalatin wa-kulli shiddatin wa-baliyyat. Yā Subbūḥ, yā Quddūs, yā rabbal-malā’ikati wal-rūḥ. Wa-ṣalla-Allāhu ‘alā sayyidinā Muḥammad wa-‘alā ālihi wa-ṣaḥbihi wa-sallam.

O Allah, You who all of this belongs to—the gracious throne, the eternal dominion, the overwhelming gifts, the great favor, and the straight path. O You who are the sender of wind. O You who are the One who causes the dawn to break. O You who are the One who resurrects all souls. O You who are the benefactor and the mercifully lenient. O Allah, O Allah, O Allah. O Compassionate,

O Compassionate, O Compassionate. O Singular, O Eternally Absolute. O You who are unique, O You who are One. O You who are Living. O You who are Self-Subsisting. O You who are the Lord of Majesty and Bounty. Be merciful in the face of our humble imperfection, our poverty, our need, our submission, our devotion in Your presence, our reliance on You, and our pleading to You. Our Lord, make every difficult matter easy and protect us from the evil of every unjust human, every envier, every harm and deformity, every disease and trial, every epidemic and plague, every earthquake, and every difficult matter and trial. O You who are the One worthy of praise. O Holy One. O You who are Lord of the angels and the archangel. And may Allah send his prayers and peace upon Prophet Muhammad and upon the family and companions of Prophet Muhammad.

﴿ وَلَوْ أَنَّنَا نَزَّلْنَآ إِلَيْهِمُ ٱلْمَلَـٰٓئِكَةَ وَكَلَّمَهُمُ ٱلْمَوْتَىٰ وَحَشَرْنَا عَلَيْهِمْ كُلَّ شَىْءٍ قُبُلًا مَّا كَانُوا۟ لِيُؤْمِنُوٓا۟ إِلَّآ أَن يَشَآءَ ٱللَّهُ وَلَـٰكِنَّ أَكْثَرَهُمْ يَجْهَلُونَ ۝

Wa-law annanā nazzalnā ilayhimul-malā'ikata wa-kallamahumul-mawtā wa-ḥasharnā 'alayhim kulla shay'in qubulan mā kānū li-yu'minū illā an yashā'a-Allāhu wa-lākinna aktharahum yajhalūn.

Even if We had sent them the angels, made the dead speak to them, and assembled before their own eyes every sign [they demanded], they still would not have believed—unless Allah so willed. But most of them are ignorant [of this].

وَكَذَٰلِكَ جَعَلْنَا لِكُلِّ نَبِيٍّ عَدُوًّا شَيَاطِينَ ٱلْإِنسِ وَٱلْجِنِّ يُوحِى بَعْضُهُمْ إِلَىٰ بَعْضٍ زُخْرُفَ ٱلْقَوْلِ غُرُورًا وَلَوْ شَآءَ رَبُّكَ مَا فَعَلُوهُ فَذَرْهُمْ وَمَا يَفْتَرُونَ ۝

⟨112⟩ Wa-ka-dhālika ja‘alnā li-kulli nabiyyin ‘aduwwan shayāṭīnal-insi wal-jinni yūḥī ba‘ḍuhum ilā ba‘ḍin zukhrufal-qawli ghurūran wa-law shā’a rabbuka mā fa‘alūhu fa-dharhum wa-mā yaftarūn.

⟨112⟩ And so We have made for every prophet enemies—devilish humans and jinn—whispering to one another with elegant words of deception. Had it been your Lord's Will, they would not have done such a thing. So leave them and their deceit.

وَلِتَصْغَىٰ إِلَيْهِ أَفْئِدَةُ ٱلَّذِينَ لَا يُؤْمِنُونَ بِٱلْآخِرَةِ وَلِيَرْضَوْهُ وَلِيَقْتَرِفُوا۟ مَا هُم مُّقْتَرِفُونَ ۝

⟨113⟩ Wa-li-taṣghā ilayhi af’idatu-lladhīna lā yu’minūna bil-ākhirati wa-li-yarḍawhu wa-li-yaqtarifū mā hum muqtarifūn.

⟨113⟩ So that the hearts of those who disbelieve in the Hereafter may be receptive to it, be pleased with it, and be persistent in their evil pursuits.

أَفَغَيْرَ ٱللَّهِ أَبْتَغِى حَكَمًا وَهُوَ ٱلَّذِىٓ أَنزَلَ إِلَيْكُمُ ٱلْكِتَٰبَ مُفَصَّلًا وَٱلَّذِينَ ءَاتَيْنَٰهُمُ ٱلْكِتَٰبَ يَعْلَمُونَ أَنَّهُۥ مُنَزَّلٌ مِّن رَّبِّكَ بِٱلْحَقِّ فَلَا تَكُونَنَّ مِنَ ٱلْمُمْتَرِينَ ۝

114 *A-fa-ghayra-Allāhi abtaghī ḥakaman wa-huwa-lladhī anzala ilaykumul-kitāba mufaṣṣalan wa-lladhīna ātaynāhumul-kitāba yaʿlamūna annahu munazzalun mir-rabbika bil-ḥaqqi fa-lā takūnanna minal-mumtarīn.*

114 [Say, O Prophet,] "Should I seek a judge other than Allah while He is the One who has revealed for you the Book [with the truth] perfectly explained?" Those who were given the Scripture know that it has been revealed [to you] from your Lord in truth. So do not be one of those who doubt.

◆─◆

وَتَمَّتْ كَلِمَتُ رَبِّكَ صِدْقًا وَعَدْلًا لَّا مُبَدِّلَ لِكَلِمَٰتِهِۦ وَهُوَ ٱلسَّمِيعُ ٱلْعَلِيمُ ۝

115 *Wa-tammat kalimatu rabbika ṣidqan wa-ʿadlan lā mubaddila li-kalimātihi wa-huwas-samīʿul-ʿalīm.*

115 The Word of your Lord has been perfected in truth and justice. None can change His Words. And He is the All-Hearing, All-Knowing.

◆─◆

وَإِن تُطِعْ أَكْثَرَ مَن فِي ٱلْأَرْضِ يُضِلُّوكَ عَن سَبِيلِ ٱللَّهِ إِن يَتَّبِعُونَ
إِلَّا ٱلظَّنَّ وَإِنْ هُمْ إِلَّا يَخْرُصُونَ ﴿١١٦﴾

⑯ *Wa-in tuṭi' akthara man fil-arḍi yuḍillūka 'an sabīli-llāhi in
yattabi'ūna illaẓ-ẓanna wa-in hum illā yakhruṣūn.*

⑯ [O Prophet!] If you were to obey most of those on earth, they
would lead you away from Allah's Way. They follow nothing but
assumptions and do nothing but lie.

◆━◆

إِنَّ رَبَّكَ هُوَ أَعْلَمُ مَن يَضِلُّ عَن سَبِيلِهِۦ وَهُوَ أَعْلَمُ بِٱلْمُهْتَدِينَ ﴿١١٧﴾

⑰ *Inna rabbaka huwa a'lamu man yaḍillu 'an sabīlihi wa-huwa
a'lamu bil-muhtadīn.*

⑰ Indeed, your Lord knows best who has strayed from His Way
and who is [rightly] guided.

◆━◆

فَكُلُوا۟ مِمَّا ذُكِرَ ٱسْمُ ٱللَّهِ عَلَيْهِ إِن كُنتُم بِـَٔايَٰتِهِۦ مُؤْمِنِينَ ﴿١١٨﴾

⑱ *Fa-kulū mimmā dhukirasmu-llāhi 'alayhi in kuntum bi-āyātihi
mu'minīn.*

⑱ So eat only of what is slaughtered in Allah's Name if you truly
believe in His revelations.

◆━◆

وَمَا لَكُمْ أَلَّا تَأْكُلُواْ مِمَّا ذُكِرَ ٱسْمُ ٱللَّهِ عَلَيْهِ وَقَدْ فَصَّلَ لَكُم مَّا حَرَّمَ عَلَيْكُمْ إِلَّا مَا ٱضْطُرِرْتُمْ إِلَيْهِ وَإِنَّ كَثِيرًا لَّيُضِلُّونَ بِأَهْوَآئِهِم بِغَيْرِ عِلْمٍ إِنَّ رَبَّكَ هُوَ أَعْلَمُ بِٱلْمُعْتَدِينَ ۝

(119) *Wa-mā lakum allā ta'kulū mimmā dhukirasmu-llāhi ʿalayhi wa-qad faṣṣala lakum mā ḥarrama ʿalaykum illā ma-ḍṭurirtum ilayhi wa-inna kathīral la-yuḍillūna bi-ahwāʾihim bi-ghayri ʿilmin inna rabbaka huwa aʿlamu bil-muʿtadīn.*

(119) Why should you not eat of what is slaughtered in Allah's Name when He has already explained to you what He has forbidden to you—except when compelled by necessity? Many [deviants] certainly mislead others by their whims out of ignorance. Surely your Lord knows the transgressors best.

◆━◆

وَذَرُواْ ظَٰهِرَ ٱلْإِثْمِ وَبَاطِنَهُ إِنَّ ٱلَّذِينَ يَكْسِبُونَ ٱلْإِثْمَ سَيُجْزَوْنَ بِمَا كَانُواْ يَقْتَرِفُونَ ۝

(120) *Wa-dharū ẓāhiral-ithmi wa-bāṭinah inna-lladhīna yaksibūnal-ithma sayujzawna bimā kānū yaqtarifūn.*

(120) Shun all sin—open and secret. Indeed, those who commit sin will be punished for what they earn.

◆━◆

وَلَا تَأْكُلُوا مِمَّا لَمْ يُذْكَرِ اسْمُ اللَّهِ عَلَيْهِ وَإِنَّهُ لَفِسْقٌ وَإِنَّ الشَّيَاطِينَ لَيُوحُونَ إِلَىٰ أَوْلِيَآئِهِمْ لِيُجَادِلُوكُمْ وَإِنْ أَطَعْتُمُوهُمْ إِنَّكُمْ لَمُشْرِكُونَ ۝

(121) *Wa-lā ta'kulū mimmā lam yudhkar-ismu-llāhi 'alayhi wa-innahu la-fisq wa-innash-shayāṭīna la-yūḥūna ilā awliyā'ihim li-yujādilūkum wa-in aṭa'tumūhum innakum la-mushrikūn.*

(121) Do not eat of what is not slaughtered in Allah's Name. For that would certainly be [an act of] disobedience. Surely the devils whisper to their [human] associates to argue with you. If you were to obey them, then you [too] would be polytheists.

◆━◆◆━◆

أَوَمَن كَانَ مَيْتًا فَأَحْيَيْنَاهُ وَجَعَلْنَا لَهُ نُورًا يَمْشِي بِهِ فِي النَّاسِ كَمَن مَّثَلُهُ فِي الظُّلُمَاتِ لَيْسَ بِخَارِجٍ مِّنْهَا كَذَٰلِكَ زُيِّنَ لِلْكَافِرِينَ مَا كَانُوا يَعْمَلُونَ ۝

(122) *A-wa-man kāna maytan fa-aḥyaynāhu wa-ja'alnā lahu nūran yamshī bihi fin-nāsi ka-man mathaluhu fiẓ-ẓulumāti laysa bi-khārijim-minhā ka-dhālika zuyyina lil-kāfirīna mā kānū ya'malūn.*

(122) Can those who had been dead, to whom We gave life and a light with which they can walk among people, be compared to those in complete darkness from which they can never emerge? That is how the misdeeds of the disbelievers have been made appealing to them.

◆━◆◆━◆

وَكَذَٰلِكَ جَعَلْنَا فِي كُلِّ قَرْيَةٍ أَكَابِرَ مُجْرِمِيهَا لِيَمْكُرُوا۟ فِيهَا ۖ وَمَا يَمْكُرُونَ إِلَّا بِأَنفُسِهِمْ وَمَا يَشْعُرُونَ ۝

(123) *Wa-ka-dhālika ja'alnā fī kulli qaryatin ākābira mujrimīhā li-yamkurū fīhā wa-mā yamkurūna illā bi-anfusihim wa-mā yash'urūn.*

(123) And so We have placed in every society the most wicked to conspire in it. Yet they plot only against themselves, but they fail to perceive it.

◆—◆—◆

وَإِذَا جَآءَتْهُمْ ءَايَةٌ قَالُوا۟ لَن نُّؤْمِنَ حَتَّىٰ نُؤْتَىٰ مِثْلَ مَآ أُوتِيَ رُسُلُ ٱللَّهِ ... ۝

(124) *Wa-idhā jā'athum āyatun qālū lan nu'mina ḥattā nu'tā mithla mā ūtiya rusulu-llāhi ...*

(124) Whenever a sign comes to them, they say, "We will never believe until we receive what Allah's messengers received" ...

Pause here and read 41 times

﴿ رَبَّنَا ءَامَنَّا بِمَآ أَنزَلْتَ وَٱتَّبَعْنَا ٱلرَّسُولَ فَٱكْتُبْنَا مَعَ ٱلشَّهِدِينَ ﴾

❀ *Rabbanā āmannā bimā anzalta wa-ttaba'nar-rasūla fa-ktubnā ma'ash-shāhidīn.* ❀

❀ Our Lord we have believed in what You have sent down and we have followed the Messenger, so record us with those who have borne witness to the truth. ❀

Read 41 times

﴿ وَأُفَوِّضُ أَمْرِي إِلَى ٱللَّهِ إِنَّ ٱللَّهَ بَصِيرٌ بِٱلْعِبَادِ ﴾

﴿ *Wa-ufawwiḍu amrī ila-Allāh; inna-Allāha baṣīrun bil-ʿibād.* ﴾

﴿ And I entrust my affairs to Allah; indeed
Allah is ever observant of His servants. ﴾

Read 41 times

﴿ رَبَّنَا إِنَّكَ جَامِعُ ٱلنَّاسِ لِيَوْمٍ لَّا رَيْبَ فِيهِ إِنَّ ٱللَّهَ لَا يُخْلِفُ ٱلْمِيعَادَ ﴾

﴿ *Rabbanā innaka jāmiʿun-nāsi li-yawmil-lā
rayba fīh; inna-Allāha lā yukhliful-mīʿād.* ﴾

﴿ Our Lord, You will gather people on a day in which there
is no doubt, indeed Allah does not fail in His promise. ﴾

Read

اللَّهُمَّ يَا نُورَ النُّورِ يَا مُنَوِّرَ النُّورِ يَا مُقَدِّرَ ٱلنُّورِ يَا نُورُ يَا نُورُ يَا اللّٰهُ يَا رَحْمٰنُ يَا
رَحِيمُ يَا حَيُّ يَا قَيُّومُ يَا ذَا الْجَلَلِ وَالْإِكْرَامِ.

*Allāhumma yā Nūran-nūr, yā munawwiran-nūr, yā muqaddiran-nūr,
yā Nūr, yā Nūr, yā Allāh, yā Raḥmān, yā Raḥīm, yā Ḥayy, yā Qayyūm,
yā Dhal-Jalāli wal-Ikrām.*

O Allah. You who are the light of light, the illuminator of light,
the determiner of light. O You who are the light. O You who are
the light. O Allah, O Compassionate, O Merciful, O Living, O
Self-Subsisting. O You who are the Lord of the gracious throne
and the eternal dominion.

اللَّهُمَّ افْتَحْ لَنَا أَبْوَابَ رَحْمَتِكَ وَمَغْفِرَتِكَ وَمُنَّ عَلَيْنَا بِدُخُولِ الجَنَّةِ وَأَعْتِقْنَا مِنَ النَّارِ.

Allāhumma-ftaḥ lanā abwāba raḥmatika wa-maghfiratik, wa-munna ‘alaynā bi-dukhūlil-jannat, wa-a‘tiqnā minan-nār.

O Allah, open for us the gates of Your mercy and Your forgiveness, grant us the favor of entering heaven, and free us from the fire.

إِلَهِي ضَاقَت المَذَاهِبُ إِلَّا إِلَيْكَ وَخَابَت الآمَالُ إِلَّا لَدَيْكَ وَانْقَطَعَ الرَّجَاءُ إِلَّا مِنْكَ وَبَطُلَ التَّوَكُّلُ إِلَّا عَلَيْكَ .

Ilāhī, ḍāqatal-madhāhibu illā ilayk, wa-khābatal-āmālu illā ladayk, wa-nqaṭa‘ar-rajā’u illā mink, wa-baṭulat-tawakkulu illā ‘alayk.

O God, all the paths have narrowed except for the path leading to You, all hope has been cut off except for hope in You, all our expectations have been dashed except for the expectations we have of You, and all trust has been proven false except for trust in You.

إِلَهِي مَن الَّذِي دَعَاكَ فَلَمْ تُجِبْهُ وَمَن الَّذِي اِسْتَجَارَكَ فَلَمْ تُجِرْهُ وَمَن الَّذِي سَأَلَكَ فَلَمْ تُعْطِهِ وَمَن الَّذِي اِسْتَعَانَكَ فَلَمْ تُعِنْهُ وَمَن الَّذِي تَوَكَّلَ عَلَيْكَ فَلَمْ تَكْفِهِ وَمَنْ الَّذِي اِسْتَغَاثَكَ فَلَمْ تُغِثْهُ.

Ilāhī, man alladhī da‘āka fa-lam tujibh. Wa-man alladhī-stajāraka fa-lam tujirh. Wa-man alladhi sa’alaka fa-lam tu‘ṭih. Wa-man alladhi-sta‘ānaka fa-lam tu‘inh. Wa-man alladhi tawakkala ‘alayka fa-lam takfih. Wa-man alladhi-staghāthaka fa-lam tughithh.

O God, who has ever called upon You and You didn’t respond to them? And who has ever sought shelter in You and You didn’t provide them with shelter? And who has ever asked You and You didn’t respond to them? And who has ever pleaded with You for help and You didn’t support them? And who has ever trusted You and You didn’t suffice them? And who has ever beseeched You and You didn’t save them?

وَاغَوْثَاهُ وَاغَوْثَاهُ وَاغَوْثَاهُ بِكَ أَسْتَغِيثُ بِكَ أَسْتَغِيثُ أَغِثْنَا يَا مُغِيثُ أَغِثْنَا
يَا غِيَاثَ الْمُسْتَغِيثِينَ أَغِثْنَا يَا رَجَاءَ الْمُسْتَجِيرِينَ وَيَادَلِيلَ الْمُتَحَيِّرِينَ وَيَا
صَرِيخَ الْمُسْتَصْرِخِينَ وَاسْتَجِبْ دَعْوَتَنَا يَا مُجِيبَ الدَّعَوَاتِ وَاقْضِ حَاجَاتِنَا
يَا قَاضِيَ الْحَاجَاتِ وَيَا كَافِيَ الْمُهِمَّاتِ يَا اللّٰهُ اقْضِ حَاجَاتِنَا وَحَاجَاتِ
الْحَاضِرِينَ وَحَوَائِجَ الْمُؤْمِنِينَ وَالْمُؤْمِنَاتِ وَالْمُسْلِمِينَ وَالْمُسْلِمَاتِ اللّٰهُمَّ
اسْتَجِبْ دَعَانَا وَاشْفِ مَرْضَانَا وَاصْرِفْ عَنَّا الْبَلَاءَ بِحَقِّ الْقُرْآنِ الْعَظِيمِ
وَالرَّسُولِ الْكَرِيمِ وَافْعَلْ بِنَا مَا أَنْتَ أَهْلُهُ فَإِنَّكَ أَهْلُ التَّقْوَى وَأَهْلُ الْمَغْفِرَةِ.

Wa-ghawthāh, wa-ghawthāh, wa-ghawthāh! Bika astaghīth, bika astaghīth. Aghithnā yā Mughīth, aghithnā! Yā Ghiyāthal-mustaghīthīn, aghithnā. Yā rajā'al-mustajīrīn, wa-yā dalīlal-mutaḥayyirīn, wa-yā ṣarīkhal-mustaṣrikhīn, wa-stajib da'watanā yā Mujībad-da'awāt, wa-qḍi ḥājātina yā Qāḍiyal-ḥājāt, wa-yā Kāfiyal-muhimmāt, yā Allāh, iqḍi ḥājātina wa-ḥājātil-ḥāḍirīn, wa-ḥawā'ijal-mu'minīna wal-mu'mināt, wal-muslimīna wal-muslimāt. Allāhumma-stajib du'ā'anā, wa-shfi marḍānā, wa-ṣrif 'annā al-balā'a bi-ḥaqqi al-Qur'ān al-'Aẓīm war-rasūlil-karīm, wa-f'al binā mā anta ahluh, fa-innaka ahlut-taqwā wa-ahlul-maghfira.

O Savior. O Savior. O Savior. In You I place my call for help. In You I place my call for help. Save us, O You who saves. Save us, O Savior of those calling out for help. Save us, O You who are the hope of those seeking sanctuary, the guide of those who are confused, and the destination of the cries of those crying out for help. Answer our prayers, O You who answers all prayers, and fulfill our needs, O You who fulfills all needs and who suffices in all important matters. O Allah, fulfill our needs and the needs of all those present and the needs of all believers and all Muslims. O Allah, answer our prayer, cure our sick, and move away from us all trials by the status of the great Quran and the gracious Messenger, and do with us what befits You. You are the One who deserves our piety and You are the Most Forgiving.

اللَّهُمَّ صَلِّ عَلَى سَيِّدِنَا مُحَمَّدٍ وَآلِ سَيِّدِنَا مُحَمَّدٍ اللَّهُمَّ مَتِّعْنَا بِأَسْمَاعِنَا
وَأَبْصَارِنَا وَقُوَّتِنَا مَا أَحْيَيْتَنَا وَاجْعَلْهُ الْوَارِثَ مِنَّا وَاجْعَلْ ثَأْرَنَا عَلَى مَنْ ظَلَمَنَا
وَانْصُرْنَا عَلَى مَنْ عَادَانَا وَلَا تَجْعَلْ مُصِيبَتَنَا فِي دِينِنَا وَلَا تَجْعَلِ الدُّنْيَا
أَكْبَرَ هَمِّنَا وَلَا مَبْلَغَ عِلْمِنَا وَلَا تُسَلِّطْ عَلَيْنَا مَنْ لَا يَرْحَمُنَا بِرَحْمَتِكَ يَا أَرْحَمَ
الرَّاحِمِينَ.

Allāhumma ṣalli ʿalā sayyidinā Muḥammadin wa-āli sayyidinā Muḥammad. Allāhumma matti'nā bi-asmā'inā wa-abṣārinā wa-quwwatinā mā aḥyaytanā, wa-j'alhul-wāritha minnā, wa-j'al tha'ranā ʿalā man ẓalamana, wa-nṣurnā ʿalā man ʿādānā, wa-lā taj'al muṣībatana fī dīninā, wa-lā taj'alid-dunyā akbara hamminā, wa-lā mablagha ʿilminā, wa-lā tusalliṭ ʿalaynā man lā yarḥamunā, bi-raḥmatika yā arḥamar-rāḥimīn.

O Allah, send Your prayers upon Prophet Muhammad and upon the family of Prophet Muhammad. O Allah, permit us to enjoy our hearing and our sight and our strength for as long as You keep us alive, and allow our children to be our heirs,[6] and make our revenge only against those who were unjust to us, and give us victory over those who are hostile to us. Do not try us in our faith, nor make the world the greatest of our concerns, nor the ultimate limit of our knowledge. Do not impose upon us those who would not be merciful with us—we ask you all this by Your mercy, O Most Merciful of those who show mercy.

اللَّهُمَّ ارْزُقْنَا رِزْقاً حَلَالاً طَيِّباً وَاسِعاً مُبَارَكاً وَكُنْ لَنَا عَوْناً وَمُعِيناً وَحَافِظاً
وَنَاصِراً وَأَمِيناً.

Allāhumma-rzuqnā rizqan ḥalālan ṭayyiban wāsi'an mubāraka, wa-kun lanā ʿawnan wa-mu'īnan wa-ḥāfiẓan wa-nāṣiran wa-amīna.

---

[6] Meaning allow our children (rather than more distant relatives) to be our heirs; allow us to have children and allow them to outlive us.

O Allah, grant us permissible, good, vast, blessed sustenance, and be our help, supporter, protector, granter of victory, and the One with whom our trusts are safely kept.

سُبْحَانَ الْمُنَفِّسِ عَنْ كُلِّ مَدْيُونٍ.

Subḥāna al-munaffisi ʿan kulli madyūn.

Praise be to the One who lightens the trial of those in debt.

سُبْحَانَ الْمُفَرِّجِ عَنْ كُلِّ مَحْزُونٍ.

Subḥāna al-mufarriji ʿan kulli maḥzūn.

Praise be to the One who alleviates the
trial of all those who are sad.

سُبْحَانَ مَنْ خَزَائِنُهُ بَيْنَ الْكَافِ وَالنُّونِ.

Subḥāna man khazāʾinuhu bayna al-kāf wal-nūn.

Praise be to the One who creates in the
space between Kaf and Nun.

سُبْحَانَ مَنْ إِذَا أَرَادَ شَيْئاً أَنْ يَقُولَ لَهُ كُنْ فَيَكُونُ.

Subḥāna man idhā arāda shayʾan an yaqūla lahu: kun fa-yakūn.

Praise be to the One who, if He wills something, He
but says to it, "*Kun* [Be], *fayakūn* [and it becomes]."

سُبْحَانَ الَّذِي بِيَدِهِ مَلَكُوتُ كُلِّ شَيْءٍ وَإِلَيْهِ تُرْجَعُونَ.

*Subḥāna-lladhī bi-yadihi malakūtu
kulli shayʾ, wa-ilayhi turjaʿūn.*

Praise be to the One in whose hands is the authority
over all things and to Him we shall return.

Read 7 times

يَا مُفَرِّج فَرِّجْ.

Yā Mufarrij, farrij.

O Comforter, comfort.

Read

يَا قَاضِيَ الْحَاجَاتِ يَا مُجِيبَ الدَّعَوَاتِ هَوِّنْ عَلَيْنَا كُلَّ عَسِيرٍ.

Yā Qāḍiyal-ḥājāt, yā Mujībad-da'awāt,
hawwin 'alaynā kulla 'asīr.

O fulfiller of needs, O answerer of prayers, make
easy for us everything that is difficult.

اللَّهُمَّ يَا غَنِيُّ يَا حَمِيدُ يَا مُبْدِئُ يَا مُعِيدُ يَا رَحِيمُ يَا وَدُودُ أَغْنِنِي بِحَلَالِكَ عَنْ
حَرَامِكَ وَبِفَضْلِكَ عَمَّنْ سِوَاكَ .

Allāhumma yā Ghaniyy, yā Ḥamīd, yā Mubdi', yā Mu'īd, yā Raḥīm, yā
Wadūd, aghnini bi-ḥalālika 'an ḥarāmik, wa-bi-faḍlika 'amman siwāk.

O Allah, O Sufficient, O Praiseworthy, O Originator, O Repro-
ducer, O Compassionate, O Loving, free me from the need for
prohibited wealth through the gift of permissible wealth, free me
from the need of anyone other than You through Your favor.

يَا ذَا الْمَنِّ وَلَا يُمَنُّ عَلَيْهِ يَا مَنْ يُجِيرُ وَلَا يُجَارُ عَلَيْهِ يَا ذَا الْجَلَالِ وَالْإِكْرَامِ يَا
ذَا الطَّوْلِ وَالْإِنْعَامِ لَا إِلَهَ إِلَّا أَنْتَ يَا ظَهْرَ اللَّاجِئِينَ سُبْحَانَكَ لَا إِلَهَ إِلَّا أَنْتَ يَا
أَمَانَ الْخَائِفِينَ.

Yā dhal-manni wa-lā yumannu 'alayh, yā man yujīru wa-lā yujāru
'alayh, yā dhal-jalāli wal-ikrām, yā dhaṭ-ṭawli wal-in'ām. Lā ilāha illā
ant, yā Ẓahral-lāji'īn. Subḥānak, lā ilāha illā ant, yā Amānal-khā'ifīn.

O You who grants favors and none grants Him favors. O You who grants shelter and none can withdraw His shelter. O You who are the Lord of Majesty and Bounty, there is no god other than You. O Protector of those who seek refuge, praise be to You, there is no god other than You. O safety of those who are afraid.

اللَّهُمَّ إِنْ كُنْتَ كَتَبْتَنِي فِي أُمِّ الكِتَابِ عِنْدَكَ شَقِيّاً أَوْ مَحْرُوماً أَوْ مَطْرُوداً فَثَبِّتْنِي عِنْدَكَ فِي أُمِّ الكِتَابِ سَعِيدَ الدَّارَيْنِ مَرْزُوقاً مُوَفَّقاً لِلْخَيْرَاتِ يَامَنْ قُلْتَ وَقَوْلُكَ الحَقّ سُبْحَانَكَ :

﴿ يَمْحُواْ ٱللَّهُ مَا يَشَآءُ وَيُثْبِتُ وَعِندَهُۥ أُمُّ ٱلْكِتَٰبِ ﴾

Allāhumma in kunta katabtanī fī Ummil-Kitābi ‘indaka shaqiyyan aw maḥrūman aw maṭrūda, fa-thabbitnī ‘indaka fī Ummil-Kitābi sa‘īdad-dārayn, marzūqan muwaffaqan lil-khayrāt. Yā man qulta wa-qawlukal-ḥaqq:

﴿ Yamḥu-llāhu mā yashā’u wa-yuthbit, wa-‘indahu Ummul-Kitāb. ﴾

O Allah, if You have recorded me in the Mother of the Book as one who is miserable, deprived, or cast out, then confirm me as one who is pleased, provided for, and guided to all that is good. O You who have said—and Your words are true:

﴿ Allah erases what He wills and confirms [what He wills]. And with Him is the Mother of the Book. ﴾

اللَّهُمَّ دَعَوْنَاكَ كَمَا أَمَرْتَنَا فَاسْتَجِبْ لَنَا كَمَا وَعَدْتَنَا.

Allāhumma da‘awnāka kamā amartanā, fa-stajib lanā kamā wa‘adtanā.

We call upon You, O Allah, as You have ordered us, so respond to us as You have promised us.

Then read

يَا حَيُّ يَا قَيُّومُ يَا بَدِيعَ السَّمَوَاتِ وَالأَرْضِ يَا ذَا الجَلَالِ وَالإِكْرَامِ فَرِّجْ عَنَّا مَا نَحْنُ فِيهِ مِنَ الضِّيقِ يَا قَدِيمَ الإِحْسَانِ وَيَا حَنَّانُ وَيَا مَنَّانُ يَا دَائِمَ الإِحْسَانِ لَا إِلَهَ إِلَّا أَنْتَ سَاتِرٌ وَجَابِرُ الكَسْرِ ارْحَمْ فَقْرَنَا إِلَيْكَ وَيَسِّر لَنَا أُمُورَنَا وَارْزُقْنَا رِزْقاً حَلَالاً وَاسِعاً مِنْ عِنْدِكَ تَهْدِي بِهِ قُلُوبَنَا وَتُغْنِي بِهِ فَقْرَنَا وَتَقْطَع بِهِ عَلَائِقَ الشَّيْطَانِ مِنْ قُلُوبِنَا إِنَّكَ أَنْتَ الحَنَّانُ الوَهَّابُ الرَّزَّاقُ الفَتَّاحُ العَلِيمُ البَاسِطُ الجَوَادُ الكَافِي الغَنِيُّ المُغْنِي الكَرِيمُ المُعْطِي الوَاسِعُ الشَّكُور ذُو الفَضْلِ وَالنِّعَمِ وَالجُودِ وَالكَرَمِ.

Yā Ḥayy, yā Qayyūm, yā Badī'as-samāwāti wal-arḍ, yā dhal-jalāli wal-ikrām, farrij 'annā mā naḥnu fīhi minaḍ-ḍīq. Yā Qadīmal-iḥsān, wa-yā ḥannān, wa-yā Mannān, yā Dā'imal-iḥsān. Lā ilāha illā ant, sātiru wa-jābirul-kasr, irḥam faqranā ilayk, wa-yassir lanā umūranā, wa-rzuqnā rizqan ḥalālan wāsi'an min 'indik, tahdī bihi qulūbanā, wa-tughni bihi faqranā, wa-taqṭā' bihi 'alā'iqash-shayṭāni min qulūbinā. Innaka anta al-Ḥannān, al-Wahhāb, ar-Razzāq, al-Fattāḥ, al-'Alīm, al-Bāsiṭ, al-Jawād, al-Kāfī, al-Ghaniyy, al-Mughnī, al-Karīm, al-Mu'ṭī, al-Wāsi', ash-Shakūr, dhūl-faḍli wan-ni'ami wal-jūdi wal-karam.

O Living, O Self-Subsisting, O Creator of the heavens and of the earth, O Lord of Majesty and Bounty, alleviate the distress we are in. O You whose beneficence is eternal, O You who are ever compassionate and constantly showing favor, O You whose beneficence is constant. There is no god other than You. O You who are the Concealer and the Healer of what is broken within us, be merciful with our dire need for You, facilitate our affairs, and grant us a permissible, vast sustenance from You through which You guide our hearts and replace our poverty with wealth. Cut off from our hearts the clinging threads of Satan, O You who are the Ever Compassionate, the Bestower, the Sustainer, the Opener, the All-Knowing, the Gracious Giver, the One who Suffices, the Expander, the Sufficient, the Enricher, the Generous, the Giver, the Vast, the Grateful, the One full of favors, blessings, gracious giving, and generosity.

وَٱللَّهُ أَعْلَمُ حَيْثُ يَجْعَلُ رِسَالَتَهُۥ سَيُصِيبُ ٱلَّذِينَ أَجْرَمُواْ صَغَارٌ ... عِندَ ٱللَّهِ وَعَذَابٌ شَدِيدٌۢ بِمَا كَانُواْ يَمْكُرُونَ ﴿١٢٤﴾

⟨124⟩ *... Allāhu aʿlamu ḥaythu yajʿalu risālatah sayuṣību-lladhīna ajramū ṣaghārun ʿinda-Allāhi wa-ʿadhābun shadīdun bi-mā kānū yamkurūn.*

⟨124⟩ ... Allah knows best where to place His message. The wicked will soon be overwhelmed by humiliation from Allah and a severe punishment for their evil plots.

◆━◆◆━◆

فَمَن يُرِدِ ٱللَّهُ أَن يَهْدِيَهُۥ يَشْرَحْ صَدْرَهُۥ لِلْإِسْلَمِ وَمَن يُرِدْ أَن يُضِلَّهُۥ يَجْعَلْ صَدْرَهُۥ ضَيِّقًا حَرَجًا كَأَنَّمَا يَصَّعَّدُ فِى ٱلسَّمَآءِ كَذَلِكَ يَجْعَلُ ٱللَّهُ ٱلرِّجْسَ عَلَى ٱلَّذِينَ لَا يُؤْمِنُونَ ﴿١٢٥﴾

⟨125⟩ *Fa-man yuridi-llāhu an yahdiyahu yashraḥ ṣadrahu lil-islāmi wa-man yurid an yuḍillahu yajʿal ṣadrahu ḍayyiqan ḥarajan ka-annamā yaṣṣaʿʿadu fis-samāʾi ka-dhālika yajʿalu-llāhur-rijsa ʿalā-lladhīna lā yuʾminūn.*

⟨125⟩ Whoever Allah wills to guide, He opens their heart to Islam. But whoever He wills to leave astray, He makes their chest tight and constricted as if they were climbing up into the sky. This is how Allah dooms those who disbelieve.

◆━◆◆━◆

وَهَـٰذَا صِرَٰطُ رَبِّكَ مُسْتَقِيمًا قَدْ فَصَّلْنَا ٱلْأَيَـٰتِ لِقَوْمٍ يَذَّكَّرُونَ ﴿١٢٦﴾

⟨126⟩ *Wa-hādhā ṣirāṭu rabbika mustaqīman qad faṣṣalnal-āyāti li-qawmin yadhdhakkarūn.*

⟨126⟩ That is your Lord's Path—perfectly straight. We have already made the signs clear to those who are mindful.

﴿ لَهُمْ دَارُ ٱلسَّلَـٰمِ عِندَ رَبِّهِمْ ۖ وَهُوَ وَلِيُّهُم بِمَا كَانُوا۟ يَعْمَلُونَ ۱۲۷ ﴾

(127) *Lahum dārus-salāmi 'inda rabbihim wa-huwa walīyyuhum bi-mā kānū ya'malūn.*

(127) They will have the Home of Peace with their Lord, who will be their Guardian because of what they used to do.

وَيَوْمَ يَحْشُرُهُمْ جَمِيعًا يَـٰمَعْشَرَ ٱلْجِنِّ قَدِ ٱسْتَكْثَرْتُم مِّنَ ٱلْإِنسِ ۖ وَقَالَ أَوْلِيَآؤُهُم مِّنَ ٱلْإِنسِ رَبَّنَا ٱسْتَمْتَعَ بَعْضُنَا بِبَعْضٍ وَبَلَغْنَآ أَجَلَنَا ٱلَّذِىٓ أَجَّلْتَ لَنَا ۚ قَالَ ٱلنَّارُ مَثْوَىٰكُمْ خَـٰلِدِينَ فِيهَآ إِلَّا مَا شَآءَ ٱللَّهُ ۗ إِنَّ رَبَّكَ حَكِيمٌ عَلِيمٌ ۱۲۸

(128) *Wa-yawma yaḥshuruhum jamī'an yā ma'sharal-jinni qad istakthartum-minal-insi wa-qāla awliyā'uhum minal-insi rabbana-stamta'a ba'ḍunā bi-ba'ḍin wa-balaghnā ajalana-lladhī ajjalta lanā qāla al-nāru mathwākum khālidīna fīhā illā mā shā'a-Allāhu inna rabbaka ḥakīmun 'alīm.*

(128) [Consider] the Day He will gather them [all] together and say, "O assembly of jinn! You misled humans in great numbers." And their human associates will say, "Our Lord! We benefited from each other's company, but now we have reached the term which You appointed for us." [Then] He will say, "The Fire is your home, yours to stay in forever, except whoever Allah wills to spare." Surely your Lord is All-Wise, All-Knowing.

وَكَذَٰلِكَ نُوَلِّي بَعْضَ ٱلظَّٰلِمِينَ بَعْضًا بِمَا كَانُواْ يَكْسِبُونَ ۝

⟨129⟩ *Wa-ka-dhālika nuwallī baʿḍaẓ-ẓālimīna baʿḍan bi-mā kānū yaksibūn.*

⟨129⟩ This is how We make the wrongdoers [destructive] allies of one another because of their misdeeds.

يَٰمَعْشَرَ ٱلْجِنِّ وَٱلْإِنسِ أَلَمْ يَأْتِكُمْ رُسُلٌ مِّنكُمْ يَقُصُّونَ عَلَيْكُمْ ءَايَٰتِي وَيُنذِرُونَكُمْ لِقَآءَ يَوْمِكُمْ هَٰذَا قَالُواْ شَهِدْنَا عَلَىٰٓ أَنفُسِنَا وَغَرَّتْهُمُ ٱلْحَيَوٰةُ ٱلدُّنْيَا وَشَهِدُواْ عَلَىٰٓ أَنفُسِهِمْ أَنَّهُمْ كَانُواْ كَٰفِرِينَ ۝

⟨130⟩ *Yā maʿsharal-jinni wal-insi a-lam yaʾtikum rusulun minkum yaquṣṣūna ʿalaykum āyātī wa-yundhirūnakum liqāʾa yawmikum hādhā qālū shahidnā ʿalā anfusinā wa-gharrathumul-ḥayātud-dunyā wa-shahidū ʿalā anfusihim annahum kānū kāfirīn.*

⟨130⟩ [Allah will ask,] "O assembly of jinn and humans! Did messengers not come from among you, proclaiming My revelations and warning you of the coming of this Day of yours?" They will say, "We confess against ourselves!" For they have been deluded by [their] worldly life. And they will testify against themselves that they were disbelievers.

ذَٰلِكَ أَن لَّمْ يَكُن رَّبُّكَ مُهْلِكَ ٱلْقُرَىٰ بِظُلْمٍ وَأَهْلُهَا غَٰفِلُونَ ۝

⟨131⟩ *Dhālika al-lam yakur-rabbuka muhlikal-qurā bi-ẓulmin wa-ahluhā ghāfilūn.*

⟨131⟩ This [sending of the messengers] is because your Lord would never destroy a society for their wrongdoing while its people are unaware [of the truth].

وَلِكُلٍّ دَرَجَـٰتٌ مِّمَّا عَمِلُوا۟ وَمَا رَبُّكَ بِغَـٰفِلٍ عَمَّا يَعْمَلُونَ ﴿١٣٢﴾

⟨132⟩ *Wa-li-kullin darajātun mimmā ‘amilū wa-mā rabbuka bi-ghāfilin ‘ammā ya‘malūn.*

⟨132⟩ They will each be assigned ranks according to their deeds. And your Lord is not unaware of what they do.

◆━━◆

وَرَبُّكَ ٱلْغَنِيُّ ذُو ٱلرَّحْمَةِ إِن يَشَأْ يُذْهِبْكُمْ وَيَسْتَخْلِفْ مِنۢ بَعْدِكُم مَّا يَشَآءُ كَمَآ أَنشَأَكُم مِّن ذُرِّيَّةِ قَوْمٍ ءَاخَرِينَ ﴿١٣٣﴾

⟨133⟩ *Wa-rabbukal-ghaniyyu dhur-raḥma in yasha’ yudh-hibkum wa-yastakhlif min ba‘dikum mā yashā’u kamā ansha’akum min dhurriyyati qawmin ākharīn.*

⟨133⟩ Your Lord is the Self-Sufficient, Full of Mercy. If He wills, He can do away with you and replace you with whoever He wills, just as He produced you from the offspring of other people.

◆━━◆

إِنَّ مَا تُوعَدُونَ لَآتٍ وَمَآ أَنتُم بِمُعْجِزِينَ ﴿١٣٤﴾

⟨134⟩ *Inna mā tū‘adūna la-ātin wa-mā antum bi-mu‘jizīn.*

⟨134⟩ Indeed, what you have been promised will certainly come to pass. And you will have no escape.

◆━━◆

قُل يَٰقَوْمِ ٱعْمَلُواْ عَلَىٰ مَكَانَتِكُمْ إِنِّي عَامِلٌ فَسَوْفَ تَعْلَمُونَ مَن تَكُونُ لَهُۥ عَٰقِبَةُ ٱلدَّارِ إِنَّهُۥ لَا يُفْلِحُ ٱلظَّٰلِمُونَ ۝١٣٥

(135) *Qul yā qawmi-‘malū ‘alā makānatikum innī ‘āmilun fa-sawfa ta‘lamūna man takūnu lahu ‘āqibatud-dāri innahu lā yufliḥuẓ-ẓālimūn.*

(135) Say, [O Prophet,] "O my people! Persist in your ways, for I [too] will persist in mine. You will soon know who will fare best in the end. Indeed, the wrongdoers will never succeed."

وَجَعَلُواْ لِلَّهِ مِمَّا ذَرَأَ مِنَ ٱلْحَرْثِ وَٱلْأَنْعَٰمِ نَصِيبًا فَقَالُواْ هَٰذَا لِلَّهِ بِزَعْمِهِمْ وَهَٰذَا لِشُرَكَآئِنَا فَمَا كَانَ لِشُرَكَآئِهِمْ فَلَا يَصِلُ إِلَى ٱللَّهِ وَمَا كَانَ لِلَّهِ فَهُوَ يَصِلُ إِلَىٰ شُرَكَآئِهِمْ سَآءَ مَا يَحْكُمُونَ ۝١٣٦

(136) *Wa-ja‘alū li-llāhi mimmā dhara’a minal-ḥarthi wal-an‘āmi naṣīban fa-qālū hādhā li-llāhi bi-za‘mihim wa-hādhā li-shurakā’inā fa-mā kāna li-shurakā’ihim fa-lā yaṣilu ila-Allāhi wa-mā kāna li-llāhi fa-huwa yaṣilu ilā shurakā’ihim sā’a mā yaḥkumūn.*

(136) The pagans set aside for Allah a share of the crops and cattle He created, saying, "This [portion] is for Allah," so they claim, "and this [one] for our associate-gods." Yet the portion of their associate-gods is not shared with Allah while Allah's portion is shared with their associate-gods. What unfair judgment!

وَكَذَٰلِكَ زَيَّنَ لِكَثِيرٍ مِّنَ ٱلْمُشْرِكِينَ قَتْلَ أَوْلَٰدِهِمْ شُرَكَآؤُهُمْ لِيُرْدُوهُمْ وَلِيَلْبِسُوا۟ عَلَيْهِمْ دِينَهُمْ وَلَوْ شَآءَ ٱللَّهُ مَا فَعَلُوهُ فَذَرْهُمْ وَمَا يَفْتَرُونَ ۝

(137) *Wa-ka-dhālika zayyana li-kathīrin minal-mushrikīna qatla awlādihim shurakā'uhum li-yurdūhum wa-liyalbisū 'alayhim dīnahum wa-law shā'a-Allāhu mā fa'alūhu fa-dharhum wa-mā yaftarūn.*

(137) Likewise, the pagans' evil associates have made it appealing to them to kill their own children—only leading to their destruction as well as confusion in their faith. Had it been Allah's Will, they would not have done such a thing. So leave them and their falsehood.

وَقَالُوا۟ هَٰذِهِۦ أَنْعَٰمٌ وَحَرْثٌ حِجْرٌ لَّا يَطْعَمُهَآ إِلَّا مَن نَّشَآءُ بِزَعْمِهِمْ وَأَنْعَٰمٌ حُرِّمَتْ ظُهُورُهَا وَأَنْعَٰمٌ لَّا يَذْكُرُونَ ٱسْمَ ٱللَّهِ عَلَيْهَا ٱفْتِرَآءً عَلَيْهِ سَيَجْزِيهِم بِمَا كَانُوا۟ يَفْتَرُونَ ۝

(138) *Wa-qālū hādhihi an'āmun wa-ḥarthun ḥijrun lā yaṭ'amuhā illā man nashā'u bi-za'mihim wa-an'āmun ḥurrimat ẓuhūruhā wa-an'āmul-lā yadhkurūnasma-Allāhi 'alayha-ftirā'an 'alayhi sayajzīhim bimā kānū yaftarūn.*

(138) They say, "These cattle and crops are reserved—none may eat them except those we permit," so they claim. Some other cattle are exempted from labor and others are not slaughtered in Allah's Name—falsely attributing lies to Him. He will repay them for their lies.

وَقَالُواْ مَا فِي بُطُونِ هَٰذِهِ ٱلْأَنْعَٰمِ خَالِصَةٌ لِّذُكُورِنَا وَمُحَرَّمٌ عَلَىٰٓ أَزْوَٰجِنَا وَإِن يَكُن مَّيْتَةً فَهُمْ فِيهِ شُرَكَآءُ سَيَجْزِيهِمْ وَصْفَهُمْ إِنَّهُۥ حَكِيمٌ عَلِيمٌ ۝١٣٩

(139) Wa-qālū mā fī buṭūni hādhihil-anʿāmi khāliṣatul-li-dhukūrina wa-muḥarramun ʿalā azwājinā wa-in yakum-maytatan fa-hum fīhi shurakāʾ sayajzīhim waṣfahum innahu ḥakīmun ʿalīm.

(139) They [also] say, "The offspring of this cattle is reserved for our males and forbidden to our females; but if it is stillborn, they may all share it." He will repay them for their falsehood. Surely He is All-Wise, All-Knowing.

◆—◼—◆

قَدْ خَسِرَ ٱلَّذِينَ قَتَلُوٓاْ أَوْلَٰدَهُمْ سَفَهًۢا بِغَيْرِ عِلْمٍ وَحَرَّمُواْ مَا رَزَقَهُمُ ٱللَّهُ ٱفْتِرَآءً عَلَى ٱللَّهِ قَدْ ضَلُّواْ وَمَا كَانُواْ مُهْتَدِينَ ۝١٤٠

(140) Qad khasira-lladhīna qatalū awlādahum safahan bi-ghayri ʿilmin wa-ḥarramū mā razaqahumu-llāhu-ftirāʾan ʿala-Allāhi qad ḍallū wa-mā kānū muhtadīn.

(140) Lost indeed are those who have murdered their own children foolishly out of ignorance and have forbidden what Allah has provided for them—falsely attributing lies to Allah. They have certainly strayed and are not [rightly] guided.

◆—◼—◆

* وَهُوَ ٱلَّذِىٓ أَنشَأَ جَنَّـٰتٍ مَّعْرُوشَـٰتٍ وَغَيْرَ مَعْرُوشَـٰتٍ وَٱلنَّخْلَ وَٱلزَّرْعَ مُخْتَلِفًا أُكُلُهُۥ وَٱلزَّيْتُونَ وَٱلرُّمَّانَ مُتَشَـٰبِهًا وَغَيْرَ مُتَشَـٰبِهٍۚ كُلُوا۟ مِن ثَمَرِهِۦٓ إِذَآ أَثْمَرَ وَءَاتُوا۟ حَقَّهُۥ يَوْمَ حَصَادِهِۦۖ وَلَا تُسْرِفُوٓا۟ إِنَّهُۥ لَا يُحِبُّ ٱلْمُسْرِفِينَ ۝

(141) *Wa-huwa-lladhī ansha'a jannātin ma'rūshātin wa-ghayra ma'rūshātin wan-nakhla waz-zar'a mukhtalifan ukuluhu waz-zaytūna war-rummāna mutashābihan wa-ghayra mutashābihin kulū min thamarihi idhā athmara wa-ātū ḥaqqahu yawma ḥaṣādihi wa-lā tusrifū innahu lā yuḥibbul-musrifīn.*

(141) He is the One who produces gardens—both cultivated and wild—and palm trees, crops of different flavors, olives, and pomegranates—similar [in shape] but dissimilar [in taste]. Eat from the fruit they bear and pay the dues at harvest, but do not waste. Surely He does not like the wasteful.

◆━━◆◆━━◆

وَمِنَ ٱلْأَنْعَـٰمِ حَمُولَةً وَفَرْشًاۚ كُلُوا۟ مِمَّا رَزَقَكُمُ ٱللَّهُ وَلَا تَتَّبِعُوا۟ خُطُوَٰتِ ٱلشَّيْطَـٰنِۚ إِنَّهُۥ لَكُمْ عَدُوٌّ مُّبِينٌ ۝

(142) *Wa-minal-an'āmi ḥamūlatan wa-farshan kulū mimmā razaqakumu-llāhu wa-lā tattabi'ū khuṭuwātish-shayṭān innahu lakum 'aduwwwum-mubīn.*

(142) Some cattle are fit for labor, others are too small. Eat of what Allah has provided for you and do not follow Satan's footsteps. Certainly, he is your sworn enemy.

◆━━◆◆━━◆

ثَمَٰنِيَةَ أَزْوَٰجٍ مِّنَ ٱلضَّأْنِ ٱثْنَيْنِ وَمِنَ ٱلْمَعْزِ ٱثْنَيْنِ قُلْ ءَآلذَّكَرَيْنِ حَرَّمَ أَمِ ٱلْأُنثَيَيْنِ أَمَّا ٱشْتَمَلَتْ عَلَيْهِ أَرْحَامُ ٱلْأُنثَيَيْنِ نَبِّئُونِى بِعِلْمٍ إِن كُنتُمْ صَٰدِقِينَ ۝

(143) *Thamāniyata azwājin minaḍ-ḍa'nith-nayni wa-minal-ma'zi-ithnayni qul ā-dhhakarayni ḥarrama amil-unthayayni amma-shtamalat 'alayhi arḥāmul-unthayayni nabbi'ūnī bi-'ilmin in kuntum ṣādiqīn.*

(143) [Allah has created] four pairs: a pair of sheep and a pair of goats—ask [them, O Prophet], "Has He forbidden [to you] the two males or the two females or what is in the wombs of the two females? Tell me with knowledge, if what you say is true."

◆━◆

وَمِنَ ٱلْإِبِلِ ٱثْنَيْنِ وَمِنَ ٱلْبَقَرِ ٱثْنَيْنِ قُلْ ءَآلذَّكَرَيْنِ حَرَّمَ أَمِ ٱلْأُنثَيَيْنِ أَمَّا ٱشْتَمَلَتْ عَلَيْهِ أَرْحَامُ ٱلْأُنثَيَيْنِ أَمْ كُنتُمْ شُهَدَآءَ إِذْ وَصَّىٰكُمُ ٱللَّهُ بِهَٰذَا فَمَنْ أَظْلَمُ مِمَّنِ ٱفْتَرَىٰ عَلَى ٱللَّهِ كَذِبًا لِّيُضِلَّ ٱلنَّاسَ بِغَيْرِ عِلْمٍ إِنَّ ٱللَّهَ لَا يَهْدِى ٱلْقَوْمَ ٱلظَّٰلِمِينَ ۝

(144) *Wa-minal-ibili-thnayni wa-minal-baqari-thnayni qul ā-dhhakarayni ḥarrama amil-unthayayni amma-shtamalat 'alayhi arḥāmul-unthayayni am kuntum shuhadā'a idh waṣṣākumu-llāhu bihādhā fa-man aẓlamu mimman if-tarā 'ala-Allāhi kadhibal-li-yuḍillan-nāsa bi-ghayri 'ilmin inna Allāha lā yahdil-qawmaẓ-ẓālimīn.*

(144) And a pair of camels and a pair of oxen. Ask [them], "Has He forbidden [to you] the two males or the two females or what is in the wombs of the two females? Or were you present when Allah gave you this commandment?" Who does more wrong than those who fabricate lies against Allah to mislead others without [any] knowledge? Surely Allah does not guide the wrongdoing people.

قُل لَّآ أَجِدُ فِى مَآ أُوحِىَ إِلَىَّ مُحَرَّمًا عَلَىٰ طَاعِمٍ يَطْعَمُهُۥٓ إِلَّآ أَن يَكُونَ مَيْتَةً أَوْ دَمًا مَّسْفُوحًا أَوْ لَحْمَ خِنزِيرٍ فَإِنَّهُۥ رِجْسٌ أَوْ فِسْقًا أُهِلَّ لِغَيْرِ ٱللَّهِ بِهِۦ فَمَنِ ٱضْطُرَّ غَيْرَ بَاغٍ وَلَا عَادٍ فَإِنَّ رَبَّكَ غَفُورٌ رَّحِيمٌ ۝

145 *Qul lā ajidu fī mā ūḥiya ilayya muḥarraman ʿalā ṭāʿimin yaṭʿamuhu illā an yakūna maytatan aw daman masfūḥan aw laḥma khinzīrin fa-innahū rijsun aw fisqan uhilla li-ghayri-llāhi bih fa-man iḍṭurra ghayra bāghin wa-lā ʿādin fa-inna rabbaka ghafūrur-raḥīm.*

145 Say, [O Prophet,] "I do not find in what has been revealed to me anything forbidden to eat except carrion, running blood, swine—which is impure—or a sinful offering in the name of any other than Allah. But if someone is compelled by necessity—neither driven by desire nor exceeding immediate need—then surely your Lord is All-Forgiving, Most Merciful."

— ◆ —

وَعَلَى ٱلَّذِينَ هَادُواْ حَرَّمْنَا كُلَّ ذِى ظُفُرٍ وَمِنَ ٱلْبَقَرِ وَٱلْغَنَمِ حَرَّمْنَا عَلَيْهِمْ شُحُومَهُمَآ إِلَّا مَا حَمَلَتْ ظُهُورُهُمَآ أَوِ ٱلْحَوَايَآ أَوْ مَا ٱخْتَلَطَ بِعَظْمٍ ذَٰلِكَ جَزَيْنَٰهُم بِبَغْيِهِمْ وَإِنَّا لَصَٰدِقُونَ ۝

146 *Wa-ʿala-lladhīna hādū ḥarramnā kulla dhī ẓufurin wa-minal-baqari wal-ghanami ḥarramnā ʿalayhim shuḥūmahumā illā mā ḥamalat ẓuhūruhuma awil-ḥawāyā aw mākhtalaṭa bi-ʿaẓmin dhālika jazaynāhum bi-baghyihim wa-innā la-ṣādiqūn.*

146 For those who are Jewish, We forbade every animal with undivided hoofs and the fat of oxen and sheep except what is joined to their backs or intestines or mixed with bone. In this way We rewarded them for their violations. And We are certainly truthful.

فَإِن كَذَّبُوكَ فَقُل رَّبُّكُمْ ذُو رَحْمَةٍ وَاسِعَةٍ وَلَا يُرَدُّ بَأْسُهُ عَنِ ٱلْقَوْمِ ٱلْمُجْرِمِينَ ﴿١٤٧﴾

(147) *Fa-in kadhdhabūka fa-qul rabbukum dhū raḥmatin wāsi'atin wa-lā yuraddu ba'suhū anil-qawmil-mujrimīn.*

(147) But if they deny you, [O Prophet], say, "Your Lord is infinite in mercy, yet His punishment will not be averted from the wicked people."

◄—◆—►

سَيَقُولُ ٱلَّذِينَ أَشْرَكُوا لَوْ شَآءَ ٱللَّهُ مَآ أَشْرَكْنَا وَلَآ ءَابَآؤُنَا وَلَا حَرَّمْنَا مِن شَيْءٍ كَذَٰلِكَ كَذَّبَ ٱلَّذِينَ مِن قَبْلِهِم حَتَّىٰ ذَاقُوا بَأْسَنَا قُلْ هَلْ عِندَكُم مِّنْ عِلْمٍ فَتُخْرِجُوهُ لَنَا إِن تَتَّبِعُونَ إِلَّا ٱلظَّنَّ وَإِنْ أَنتُمْ إِلَّا تَخْرُصُونَ ﴿١٤٨﴾

(148) *Sayaqūlu-lladhīna ashrakū law shā'a-Allāhu mā ashraknā wa-lā ābā'unā wa-lā ḥarramnā min shay'in ka-dhālika kadhdhaba-lladhīna min qablihim ḥattā dhāqū ba'sanā qul hal 'indakum min 'ilmin fa-tukhrijūhu lanā in tattabi'ūna illāẓ-ẓanna wa-in antum illā takhrusūn.*

(148) The polytheists will argue, "Had it been Allah's Will, neither we nor our forefathers would have associated others with Him [in worship] or made anything unlawful." Likewise, those before them rejected the truth until they tasted Our punishment. Ask [them, O Prophet], "Do you have any knowledge that you can produce for us? Surely you follow nothing but [false] assumptions and you do nothing but lie."

◄—◆—►

قُل فَلِلَّهِ ٱلْحُجَّةُ ٱلْبَـٰلِغَةُ ۖ فَلَوْ شَآءَ لَهَدَىٰكُمْ أَجْمَعِينَ ۝

(149) *Qul fa-lillāhil-ḥujjatul-bālighatu fa-law shā’a la-hadākum ajma‘īn.*

(149) Say, "Allah has the most conclusive argument. Had it been His Will, He would have easily imposed guidance upon all of you."

◄❖►

قُلْ هَلُمَّ شُهَدَآءَكُمُ ٱلَّذِينَ يَشْهَدُونَ أَنَّ ٱللَّهَ حَرَّمَ هَـٰذَا ۖ فَإِن شَهِدُوا۟ فَلَا تَشْهَدْ مَعَهُمْ ۚ وَلَا تَتَّبِعْ أَهْوَآءَ ٱلَّذِينَ كَذَّبُوا۟ بِـَٔايَـٰتِنَا وَٱلَّذِينَ لَا يُؤْمِنُونَ بِٱلْـَٔاخِرَةِ وَهُم بِرَبِّهِمْ يَعْدِلُونَ ۝

(150) *Qul halumma shuhadā’akumu-lladhīna yashhadūna anna-Allāha ḥarrama hādhā fa-in shahidū fa-lā tashhad ma‘ahum wa-lā tattabi‘ ahwā’a-lladhīna kadhdhabū bi-āyātinā wa-alladhīna lā yu’minūna bil-ākhirati wa-hum bi-rabbihim ya‘dilūn.*

(150) Say, [O Prophet,] "Bring your witnesses who can testify that Allah has forbidden this." If they [falsely] testify, do not testify with them. And do not follow the desires of those who deny Our proofs, disbelieve in the Hereafter, and set up equals with their Lord.

◄❖►

۞ قُل تَعَالَوْا۟ أَتْلُ مَا حَرَّمَ رَبُّكُمْ عَلَيْكُمْ ۖ أَلَّا تُشْرِكُوا۟ بِهِۦ شَيْـًٔا ۖ وَبِٱلْوَٰلِدَيْنِ إِحْسَـٰنًا ۖ وَلَا تَقْتُلُوٓا۟ أَوْلَـٰدَكُم مِّنْ إِمْلَـٰقٍ ۖ نَّحْنُ نَرْزُقُكُمْ وَإِيَّاهُمْ ۖ وَلَا تَقْرَبُوا۟ ٱلْفَوَٰحِشَ مَا ظَهَرَ مِنْهَا وَمَا بَطَنَ ۖ وَلَا تَقْتُلُوا۟ ٱلنَّفْسَ ٱلَّتِى حَرَّمَ ٱللَّهُ إِلَّا بِٱلْحَقِّ ۚ ذَٰلِكُمْ وَصَّىٰكُم بِهِۦ لَعَلَّكُمْ تَعْقِلُونَ ۝

(151) *Qul ta'ālaw atlu mā ḥarrama rabbukum 'alaykum allā tushrikū bihi shay'an wa-bil-wālidayni iḥsānan wa-lā taqtulū awlādakum min imlāqin naḥnu narzuqukum wa-iyyāhum wa-lā taqrabūl-fawāḥisha mā ẓahara minhā wa-mā baṭana wa-lā taqtulūl-nafsa-llātī ḥarrama-Allāhu illā bil-ḥaqqi dhalikum waṣṣākum bihī la'allakum ta'qilūn.*

(151) Say, [O Prophet,] "Come! Let me recite to you what your Lord has forbidden to you: do not associate others with Him [in worship]. [Do not fail to] honor your parents. Do not kill your children for fear of poverty. We provide for you and for them. Do not come near indecencies, openly or secretly. Do not take a [human] life—made sacred by Allah—except with [legal] right. This is what He has commanded you, so perhaps you will understand.

---

(152) *Wa-lā taqrabū mālal-yatīmi illā bi-llatī hiya aḥsanu ḥattā yablugha ashuddahu wa-awful-kayla wal-mīzāna bil-qisṭi lā nukallifu nafsan illā wus'ahā wa-idhā qultum fa-'dilū wa-law kāna dhā qurba wa-bi-'ahdi-llāhi awfū dhalikum waṣṣākum bihī la'allakum tadhakkarūn.*

(152) And do not come near the wealth of the orphan—unless intending to enhance it—until they attain maturity. Give full measure and weigh with justice. We never require of any soul more than what it can afford. Whenever you speak, maintain justice—even regarding a close relative. And fulfil your covenant with Allah. This is what He has commanded you, so perhaps you will be mindful.

وَأَنَّ هَـٰذَا صِرَٰطِى مُسْتَقِيمًا فَٱتَّبِعُوهُ وَلَا تَتَّبِعُوا۟ ٱلسُّبُلَ فَتَفَرَّقَ بِكُمْ عَن سَبِيلِهِۦ ذَٰلِكُمْ وَصَّىٰكُم بِهِۦ لَعَلَّكُمْ تَتَّقُونَ ۝

(153) *Wa-anna hādhā ṣirāṭī mustaqīman fa-ttabiʿūhu wa-lā tattabiʿus-subula fa-tafarraqa bikum ʿan sabīlihi dhālikum waṣṣākum bihī laʿallakum tattaqūn.*

(153) Indeed, that is My Path—perfectly straight. So follow it and do not follow other ways, for they will lead you away from His Way. This is what He has commanded you, so perhaps you will be conscious [of Allah].”

ثُمَّ ءَاتَيْنَا مُوسَى ٱلْكِتَـٰبَ تَمَامًا عَلَى ٱلَّذِىٓ أَحْسَنَ وَتَفْصِيلًا لِّكُلِّ شَىْءٍ وَهُدًى وَرَحْمَةً لَّعَلَّهُم بِلِقَآءِ رَبِّهِمْ يُؤْمِنُونَ ۝

(154) *Thumma ātaynā Mūsal-kitāba tamāman ʿala-lladhī aḥsana wa-tafṣīlan li-kulli shay’in wa-hudan wa-raḥmatal-laʿallahum bi-liqā’i rabbihim yu’minūn.*

(154) Additionally, We gave Moses the Scripture, completing the favor upon those who do good, detailing everything, and as a guide and a mercy, so perhaps they would be certain of the meeting with their Lord.

وَهَـٰذَا كِتَـٰبٌ أَنزَلْنَـٰهُ مُبَارَكٌ فَٱتَّبِعُوهُ وَٱتَّقُوا۟ لَعَلَّكُمْ تُرْحَمُونَ ۝

(155) *Wa-hādhā kitābun anzalnāhu mubārakun fa-ttabiʿūhu wa-ttaqū laʿallakum turḥamūn.*

(155) This is a blessed Book We have revealed. So follow it and be mindful [of Allah], so you may be shown mercy.

أَن تَقُولُوٓاْ إِنَّمَآ أُنزِلَ ٱلْكِتَـٰبُ عَلَىٰ طَآئِفَتَيْنِ مِن قَبْلِنَا وَإِن كُنَّا عَن دِرَاسَتِهِمْ لَغَـٰفِلِينَ ﴿١٥٦﴾

🔊 *An taqūlū innamā unzilal-kitābu ‘alā ṭā’ifatayni min qablinā wa-in kunnā ‘an dirāsatihim la-ghāfilīn.*

🔊 You [pagans] can no longer say, "Scriptures were only revealed to two groups before us and we were unaware of their teachings."

◄━◆━◆━►

أَوْ تَقُولُواْ لَوْ أَنَّآ أُنزِلَ عَلَيْنَا ٱلْكِتَـٰبُ لَكُنَّآ أَهْدَىٰ مِنْهُمْ فَقَدْ جَآءَكُم بَيِّنَةٌ مِّن رَّبِّكُمْ وَهُدًى وَرَحْمَةٌ فَمَنْ أَظْلَمُ مِمَّن كَذَّبَ بِـَٔايَـٰتِ ٱللَّهِ وَصَدَفَ عَنْهَا سَنَجْزِى ٱلَّذِينَ يَصْدِفُونَ عَنْ ءَايَـٰتِنَا سُوٓءَ ٱلْعَذَابِ بِمَا كَانُواْ يَصْدِفُونَ ﴿١٥٧﴾

🔊 *Aw taqūlū law annā unzila ‘alaynal-kitābu la-kunnā ahdā minhum fa-qad jā’akum bayyinatum-mir-rabbikum wa-hudan wa-raḥmatun fa-man aẓlamu mimman kadhdhaba bi-āyāti-llāhi wa-ṣadafa ‘anhā sanajzi-lladhīna yaṣdifūna ‘an āyātinā sū’al-‘adhābi bimā kānū yaṣdifūn.*

🔊 Nor can you say, "If only the Scriptures had been revealed to us, we would have been better guided than they." Now there has come to you from your Lord a clear proof—a guide and mercy. Who then does more wrong than those who deny Allah's revelations and turn away from them? We will reward those who turn away from Our revelations with a dreadful punishment for turning away.

هَلْ يَنظُرُونَ إِلَّا أَن تَأْتِيَهُمُ ٱلْمَلَـٰئِكَةُ أَوْ يَأْتِيَ رَبُّكَ أَوْ يَأْتِيَ بَعْضُ ءَايَـٰتِ رَبِّكَ يَوْمَ يَأْتِي بَعْضُ ءَايَـٰتِ رَبِّكَ لَا يَنفَعُ نَفْسًا إِيمَـٰنُهَا لَمْ تَكُنْ ءَامَنَتْ مِن قَبْلُ أَوْ كَسَبَتْ فِي إِيمَـٰنِهَا خَيْرًا قُلِ ٱنتَظِرُوٓا۟ إِنَّا مُنتَظِرُونَ ۝

(158) *Hal yanẓurūna illā an ta'tiyahumul-malā'ikatu aw ya'tiya rabbuka aw ya'tiya ba'ḍu āyāti rabbika yawma ya'tī ba'ḍu āyāti rabbika lā yanfa'u nafsan īmānuhā lam takun āmanat min qablu aw kasabat fī īmānihā khayran qul intaẓirū innā muntaẓirūn.*

(158) Are they awaiting the coming of the angels, or your Lord [Himself], or some of your Lord's [major] signs? On the Day your Lord's signs arrive, belief will not benefit those who did not believe earlier or those who did no good through their faith. Say, "Keep waiting! We too are waiting."

◄━◆━►

إِنَّ ٱلَّذِينَ فَرَّقُوا۟ دِينَهُمْ وَكَانُوا۟ شِيَعًا لَّسْتَ مِنْهُمْ فِي شَىْءٍ إِنَّمَآ أَمْرُهُمْ إِلَى ٱللَّهِ ثُمَّ يُنَبِّئُهُم بِمَا كَانُوا۟ يَفْعَلُونَ ۝

(159) *Inna-lladhīna farraqū dīnahum wa-kānū shiya'al-lasta minhum fī shay'in inna mā amruhum ila-llāhi thumma yunabbi'uhum bimā kānū yaf'alūn.*

(159) Indeed, you [O Prophet] are not responsible whatsoever for those who have divided their faith and split into sects. Their judgment rests only with Allah. And He will inform them of what they used to do.

$$
\text{مَن جَآءَ بِٱلۡحَسَنَةِ فَلَهُۥ عَشۡرُ أَمۡثَالِهَاۖ وَمَن جَآءَ بِٱلسَّيِّئَةِ فَلَا يُجۡزَىٰٓ}
$$

$$
\text{إِلَّا مِثۡلَهَا وَهُمۡ لَا يُظۡلَمُونَ ۝}
$$

⑯⓪ *Man jā'a bil-ḥasanati fa-lahu 'ashru amthālihā wa-man jā'a bis-sayyi'ati fa-lā yujzā illā mithlahā wa-hum lā yuẓlamūn.*

⑯⓪ Whoever comes with a good deed will be rewarded tenfold. But whoever comes with a bad deed will be punished for only one. None will be wronged.

◆━◆

$$
\text{قُلۡ إِنَّنِي هَدَىٰنِي رَبِّي إِلَىٰ صِرَٰطٍ مُّسۡتَقِيمٍ دِينٗا قِيَمٗا مِّلَّةَ إِبۡرَٰهِيمَ حَنِيفٗا}
$$

$$
\text{وَمَا كَانَ مِنَ ٱلۡمُشۡرِكِينَ ۝}
$$

⑯① *Qul innanī hadānī rabbī ilā ṣirāṭim-mustaqīmin dīnan qiyamam-millata Ibrāhīma ḥanīfan wa-mā kāna minal-mushrikīn.*

⑯① Say, [O Prophet,] "Surely my Lord has guided me to the Straight Path, a perfect way, the faith of Abraham, the upright, who was not one of the polytheists."

◆━◆

$$
\text{قُلۡ إِنَّ صَلَاتِي وَنُسُكِي وَمَحۡيَايَ وَمَمَاتِي لِلَّهِ رَبِّ ٱلۡعَٰلَمِينَ ۝}
$$

⑯② *Qul inna ṣalātī wa-nusukī wa-maḥyāya wa-mamātī li-llāhi rabbil-'ālamīn.*

⑯② Say, "Surely my prayer, my worship, my life, and my death are all for Allah—Lord of all worlds.

لَا شَرِيكَ لَهُۥ وَبِذَٰلِكَ أُمِرْتُ وَأَنَا۠ أَوَّلُ ٱلْمُسْلِمِينَ ﴿١٦٣﴾

(163) *Lā sharīka lahu wa-bi-dhālika umirtu wa-anā awwalul-muslimīn.*

(163) He has no partner. So I am commanded, and so I am the first to submit.”

◆—◆—◆

قُلْ أَغَيْرَ ٱللَّهِ أَبْغِى رَبًّا وَهُوَ رَبُّ كُلِّ شَىْءٍ وَلَا تَكْسِبُ كُلُّ نَفْسٍ إِلَّا عَلَيْهَا وَلَا تَزِرُ وَازِرَةٌ وِزْرَ أُخْرَىٰ ثُمَّ إِلَىٰ رَبِّكُم مَّرْجِعُكُمْ فَيُنَبِّئُكُم بِمَا كُنتُمْ فِيهِ تَخْتَلِفُونَ ﴿١٦٤﴾

(164) *Qul a-ghayra-Allāhi abghī rabban wa-huwa rabbu kulli shay'in wa-lā taksibu kullu nafsin illā ʿalayhā wa-lā taziru wāziratun wizra ukh-rā thumma ilā rabbikum marjiʿukum fa-yunabbi'ukum bimā kuntum fīhi takhtalifūn.*

(164) Say, [O Prophet,] “Should I seek a lord other than Allah while He is the Lord of everything?” No one will reap except what they sow. No soul burdened with sin will bear the burden of another. Then to your Lord is your return, and He will inform you of your differences.

◆—◆—◆

وَهُوَ ٱلَّذِى جَعَلَكُمْ خَلَٰئِفَ ٱلْأَرْضِ وَرَفَعَ بَعْضَكُمْ فَوْقَ بَعْضٍ دَرَجَٰتٍ لِّيَبْلُوَكُمْ فِى مَآ ءَاتَٰكُمْ إِنَّ رَبَّكَ سَرِيعُ ٱلْعِقَابِ وَإِنَّهُۥ لَغَفُورٌ رَّحِيمٌ ﴿١٦٥﴾

(165) *Wa-huwa-lladhī jaʿalakum khalā'ifal-arḍi wa-rafāʿa baʿḍakum fawqa baʿḍin darajātil-li-yabluwakum fī mā ātākum inna rabbaka sarīʿul-ʿiqābi wa-innahu la-ghafūrur-raḥīm.*

(165) He is the One who has placed you as successors on earth and elevated some of you in rank over others, so He may test you with what He has given you. Surely your Lord is swift in punishment, but He is certainly All-Forgiving, Most Merciful.

After the Sura

After reciting the sura, make the following prayer.

Read 11 times

﴿ لَّآ إِلَهَ إِلَّآ أَنتَ سُبْحَنَكَ إِنِّي كُنتُ مِنَ ٱلظَّلِمِينَ ﴾

﴿ *Lā ilāha illā anta subḥānaka innī kuntu minaẓ-ẓālimīn.* ﴾

﴿ There is no god other than You, praise be to You, I
am among those who have wronged themselves. ﴾

Read 11 times

اَسْتَغْفِرَ اللَّهَ رَبِّي وَأَتُوبُ إِلَيْهِ.

Astaghfira-Allāha rabbī wa-atūbu ilayh.

I seek forgiveness from Allah, my Lord, and repent to Him.

Read 3 times

﴿ وَأُفَوِّضُ أَمْرِى إِلَى ٱللَّهِ إِنَّ ٱللَّهَ بَصِيرٌ بِٱلْعِبَادِ ﴾

﴿ *Wa-ufawwiḍu amrī ila-Allāh; inna-Allāha baṣīrun bil-ʿibād.* ﴾

﴿ And I entrust my affairs to Allah; indeed
Allah is ever observant of His servants. ﴾

Read 3 times

﴿ رَبَّنَا ءَاتِنَا مِن لَّدُنكَ رَحْمَةً وَهَيِّئْ لَنَا مِنْ أَمْرِنَا رَشَداً ﴾

◈ *Rabbanā ātinā mil-ladunka raḥmatan wa-*
hayyi' lanā min amrinā rashadā. ◈

◈ Our Lord, grant us mercy from Yourself and
guide us rightly through our ordeal. ◈

Read

اللَّهُمَّ صَلِّ عَلَى سَيِّدِنَا مُحَمَّدٍ وَآلِ سَيِّدِنَا مُحَمَّدٍ.

Allāhumma ṣalli 'alā sayyidinā Muḥammadin
wa āli sayyidinā Muḥammad.

O Allah, send blessings upon our Prophet
Muhammad and his family.

اَللَّهُمَّ يَا سَرِيعَ الحِسَابِ يَا شَدِيدَ العِقَابِ يَا غَفُورُ يَا رَحِيمُ يَا خَالِقَ كُلِّ شَيْءٍ
يَا رَازِقَ كُلِّ حَيٍّ يَا فَاطِرَ الأَرْضِ وَالسَّمَاءِ .

Allāhumma yā sarī'al-ḥisāb, yā shadīdal-'iqāb, yā ghafūr, yā raḥīm, yā
khāliqa kulli shay', yā rāziqa kulli ḥayy, yā fāṭiral-arḍi was-samā'.

O Allah, O Swift in reckoning, O Severe in punishment, O
Forgiving, O Merciful, O Creator of everything, O Provider for
every living being, O Originator of the earth and the heavens.

يَا فَالِقَ الْحَبِّ وَالنَّوَى يَا ذَا الْجُودِ وَالسَّمَاحِ يَا مُرْسِلَ الرِّيَاحِ يَا مُسَبِّبَ الْأَسْبَابِ يَا مُسَهِّلَ الصِّعَابِ يَا مُفَتِّحَ الْأَبْوَابِ

يَا مُدَوِّرَ الْفَلَكِ الدَّوَّارِ يَا مُقَلِّبَ الْقُلُوبِ وَالْأَبْصَارِ يَا مَنْ يَعْلَمُ الْأَسْرَارَ وَلَا يَهْتِكُ الْأَسْتَارَ يَا مُحْيِي الْأَمْوَاتِ يَا مُنَزِّلَ الْبَرَكَاتِ.

Yā fāliqal-ḥabbi wan-nawā, yā dhal-jūdi was-samāḥ, yā mursilar-riyāḥ, yā musabbibal-asbāb, yā musahhila al-ṣiʿābi, yā mufattiḥal-abwāb, yā mudawwiral-falaki al-dawwār, yā muqallibal-qulūbi wal-abṣār, yā man yaʿlamul-asrāra wa lā yahtikul-astār, yā muḥyī al-amwāt, yā munazzilal-barakāt.

O Splitter of the seed and the date stone, O Possessor of generosity and munificence, O Sender of the winds, O Causer of causes, O Facilitator of difficulties, O Opener of doors, O Turner of the revolving celestial sphere, O Turner of hearts and sights, O Knower of secrets who does not expose the veils, O Giver of life to the dead, O Sender down of blessings.

يَا نُورَ الْأَرْضِينَ وَالسَّمَاوَاتِ يَا مُقِيلَ الْعَثَرَاتِ يَا غَافِرَ الْخَطِيئَاتِ يَا سَاتِرَ الْعَوْرَاتِ يَا مَانِعَ الْبَلِيَّاتِ يَا دَافِعَ السَّيِّئَاتِ يَا كَاشِفَ الْكُرُبَاتِ يَا وَلِيَّ الْحَسَنَاتِ يَا عَالِمَ السِّرِّ وَالْخَفِيَّاتِ يَا كَافِيَ الْمُهِمَّاتِ يَا مُجِيبَ الدَّعَوَاتِ يَا قَاضِيَ الْحَاجَاتِ اقْضِ حَاجَاتِنَا وَحَاجَاتِ الْحَاضِرِينَ فِي هَذِهِ السَّاعَةِ بِحَقِّ هَذِهِ الْآيَاتِ يَا بَدِيعَ السَّمَاوَاتِ وَالْأَرْضِ يَا مَنْ لَا يَحْتَاجُ إِلَى الْبَيَانِ وَالتَّفْسِيرِ يَا إِلَهَ الْأَوَّلِينَ وَالْآخِرِينَ يَا ذَا الْجَلَالِ وَالْإِكْرَامِ اسْتَجِبْ دَعَانَا يَا سَيِّدَنَا وَمَوْلَانَا بِحَقِّ الْقُرْآنِ الْعَظِيمِ وَالنَّبِيِّ الْكَرِيمِ بِرَحْمَتِكَ يَا أَرْحَمَ الرَّاحِمِينَ وَصَلَّى اللَّهُ عَلَى سَيِّدِنَا مُحَمَّدٍ وَآلِهِ أَجْمَعِينَ.

Yā nūral-arḍin was-samāwāt, yā muqīlal-ʿatharāt, yā ghāfiral-khaṭīʾāt, yā sātiral-ʿawrāt, yā māniʿal-balīyyāt, yā dāfiʿas-sayyiʾāt, yā kāshifal-kurubāt, yā walīyyal-ḥasanāt, yā ʿālimas-sirri wal-khafiyyāt, yā kāfiyal-muhimmāt, yā mujībad-daʿawāt, yā qāḍiyal-ḥājāt, iqḍi ḥājātinā wa ḥājātil-ḥāḍirīna fī hādhihis-sāʿati biḥaqqi hādhihil-āyāt, yā badīʿas-samāwāti wal-arḍ, yā mal-lā yaḥtāju ilal-bayāni wat-tafsīr,

*yā ilāhal-awwalīna wal-ākhirīn, yā dhal-jalāli wal-ikrām, istajib
da'ānā, yā sayyidinā wa mawlānā, biḥaqqil-Qur'ānil-'aẓīmi wan-
nabīyyil-karīm, biraḥmatika yā arḥamar-rāḥimīn, wa ṣallāllāhu 'alā
sayyidinā Muḥammad wa ālihi ajma'īn.*

O Light of the earths and the heavens, O Remover of stumbles, O
Forgiver of sins, O Concealer of faults, O Preventer of calamities,
O Repeller of misdeeds, O Remover of distress, O Patron of
good deeds, O Knower of secrets and hidden things, O Sufficer
of important matters, O Answerer of supplications, O Fulfiller
of needs, fulfill our needs and the needs of those present at
this moment by the right of these verses. O Originator of the
heavens and the earth, O You who has no need for explanation
or interpretation, O God of the first and the last, O Possessor of
majesty and honor, answer our supplication, O our Master and our
Patron, by the right of the Glorious Quran and the Noble Prophet,
by Your mercy, O Most Merciful of the merciful. And may Allah
send blessings upon Prophet Muhammad and all his family.